Building a fulfilling life through your business

Your Business Journey

Workbook 1

**A 12 Month Workbook for
Women in Small Business**

Kim Chamberlain & Iona Elwood-Smith

Chrysalis for Women
www.chrysalisforwomen.com

YOUR BUSINESS JOURNEY

Address all inquiries to:

Kim Chamberlain & Iona Elwood-Smith

admin@chrysalisforwomen.com

www.chrysalisforwomen.com

ISBN: 978-0-473-41288-3

Book layout: DIYPublishing.co.nz

Every attempt has been made to properly source all quotes.

What Others are Saying about Iona, Kim and This Book

Thanks Kim and Iona for putting together such a practical and easily followed business tool. This workbook is brilliant for everyone in business, whether experienced or just starting out. It's full of wonderful prompts and exercises that get to the real bones of your business, giving you much needed clarity and focus. Once you have clarity you have inspiration and once you have inspiration everything flows.

Paula Johnson, Hired Help, www.hiredhelp.nz

Kim and Iona bring a powerful skill set, which combined with vision, focus, professionalism and a proven track record in supporting women in business, provides a pathway to success.

Alex Rodriguez, 5 Rhythms Movement Meditation Teacher, www.5rhythms.co.nz

Kim, you've been the inspiration for many of us through Chrysalis for women in business ... thanks to you.

L P Hansen, author, lphansen.com

Huge thanks Iona, with your help my business has grown over 200% this year. Your coaching is always practical, honest and packed with value. This book is the same, a fantastic small business resource.

Lesley Seabright, Creative Tuesday, www.creativetuesday.co.nz

The workbook is very good! So much useful information. It's going to be a good year for Chrysalis for Women!

Kay Drummond, Positive Personal Growth, www.positive-personal-growth.com

Following this concise workbook will not only provide you with a great practical tool for ensuring your business success but with the added benefit of you understanding who you are and how to shine in this world.

Janne Sawada

As the sole operator of my Astrology Business, I found this book Your Business Journey to be informative, practical and challenging. The information made me revise some of my business practices and I have now incorporated some new ideas from this book. A valuable read for anyone in business looking for guidance.

Christina Richter RN, Author Learn to Self-heal, www.christinastrology.com

You've got to say; I think that if I keep working at this and want it badly enough
I can have it. It's called perseverance.

Lee Iacocca

We delight in the beauty of the butterfly, but rarely admit the changes it has gone through to
achieve that beauty.

Maya Angelou

To be successful, you have to have your heart in your business, and your business in your heart.

Thomas Watson, Sr.

Success in business requires training and discipline and hard work.

But if you're not frightened by these things, the opportunities are just as great today as
they ever were.

David Rockefeller

It does not do to dwell on dreams and forget to live.

J.K. Rowling

There is nothing in a caterpillar that tells you it's going to be a butterfly.

Richard Buckminster Fuller

Do one thing every day that scares you.

Eleanor Roosevelt

DEDICATION

*For the Chrysalis women: for their generosity, their inspiration
and their drive to never stop learning and growing.*

I. E-S.

For my nan, Flo Moore, whose life attitude was 'Just get on with it'.

K.C.

ACKNOWLEDGEMENTS

We would like to thank all those who have contributed both directly or indirectly to this book:

Leanne Babcock, Jon Chamberlain, John Eaden, Sandy Geyer, Kris Lockett, Patrick Snow, Lis Sowerbutts, and all the women who have contributed to the Chrysalis for Women service.

CONTENTS

BACKGROUND

A note from Kim:

In 2013 I met a woman called Janne who had set up a small centre in Wellington where local crafts-people could sell their wares, and therapists could hire rooms to treat clients or run sessions. She described it as 'a platform to allow people to share their gifts with the world'. As my work focuses on helping people take steps forward in their personal and professional development, and as I'd been providing services for women for many years, it seemed natural to set up something together, and so the Chrysalis for Women Business Network was born — an informal network group for women in small to medium sized businesses (www.chrysalisforwomen.com). The focus has not only been on business growth and development, but also taking into account the other needs and influences we deal with as women with a business — family, friendships, the need to connect with others, our well-being, the desire to contribute, and so on.

The Chrysalis service has been running for several years, and I've been very fortunate to have had several wonderful women become involved in the running of it: Ginelle, Janne, Alex, Barbara, Kay, Willemijn and Mary; plus Iona, the co-writer of this book.

The network is constantly growing and evolving, and we've had the pleasure of watching women's businesses grow; business partnerships form, mastermind groups come about, and friendships develop.

Moving into our fourth year we decided to view the year as a business journey we would take women on via the network meetings, supported by a workbook. Hence this book. We have written it in such a way that it can be a stand-alone book for you to work through if you are not able to attend the meetings, starting at any point in the year.

Enjoy!

A note from Iona:

Over the last 18 months I have been on an incredible journey of my own. A cool new social enterprise Sub Urban Co-Working was setting up and I wanted to be part of it — but it was for businesses, and I didn't have one. With a background in start-up and small business operations I saw a gap in the market providing business support for small businesses needing strategy and direction — Grow my Business was born. As part of my own market research I joined Chrysalis for Women and met an incredible group of women — they are inspiring, and they also have an obvious need. They have helped me on my journey and I believe I have helped them.

When Kim approached me about working together I saw it as an opportunity to make a real difference in the lives of women in business and was excited to take up the challenge. As we worked on the programme and hatched the idea of the Business Journey it came together surprisingly easy as if it was waiting for us to just get on with it!

My hope is that you use the workbook to focus on the direction of your business, map your progress and take your business on a journey to where you want it to be.

Buckle up your seat belt and have a great business adventure!

INTRODUCTION

Welcome

Welcome to your business workbook; we're pleased to be accompanying you on this twelve-month journey. We'll be taking you through month by month 12 aspects that can help build your business.

This journey isn't solely about getting more business and making more money; it's also making sure you create a fulfilling, holistic life at the same time. It's about ensuring you 'satisfy your soul' while you develop a successful business.

Take a moment to draw a picture of your ideal life, showing how your business fits into that picture:

Now explain in a sentence how you would like your business to fit into your life overall:

____

____

____

____

A Fulfilling, Holistic Life

There are a number of other life areas as well as 'business' which we've put into suggested categories below. Feel free to amend these to fit in with your own life, if you prefer.

Life area	1	2	3	4	5	6	7	8	9	10
Family										
Physical health										
Social/Recreation										
Community										
Learning										
Spiritual										
Personal development										
Other										
Other										

Shade in each row to indicate how satisfied you are with each of these areas of your life, from 1 (not satisfied) to 10 (very satisfied).

Life area	Notes
Family	
Physical health	
Social/Recreation	
Community	
Learning	
Spiritual	
Personal development	
Other	
Other	

Now make some notes against each area with your thoughts on how you will maintain areas you are doing well in, or steps you'll take to improve other areas.

Sometimes when you work for yourself, the business becomes all consuming. We'll include this chart at the end of each chapter as a reminder to take care of all areas of your life.

How to Use This Book

The purpose of the workbook is to take you on a business journey over a twelve-month period.

The main section of the book contains twelve chapters — one for each month — covering a different aspect of business. Chapter 1 encompasses Goal Setting; Chapter 12 asks you to look back over the year, evaluate progress, then look towards the following year. The ten chapters in between cover some of the main aspects of developing a business.

If you are using this workbook as a stand-alone tool, feel free to work through the chapters in order, or do them in any order that works for you.

Each chapter offers

- Inspirational quotes
- An informational section on the chapter topic
- 5-minute micro actions: short activities that can bring big rewards
- Notes: A space for you to record further information on the topic that you gain from attending the network meetings, and/or carrying out your own research
- Analysis: an evaluation of where you see yourself regarding this business issue
- Your goals regarding the business issue, your timeframe and accountability method
- Results: the outcomes you have experienced
- Next step: following on from the outcomes, planning your next steps
- A time to reflect on your life areas, to ensure a fulfilling, holistic life

To gain the most from what you learn as you progress on your journey it's extremely useful to TEACH WHAT YOU LEARN. After you have read the informational section in the chapter and recorded any further information you have gleaned on the topic, teach this information to one to two people within forty-eight hours. This will ensure you look back through the information again and understand it well enough to explain it to someone else. This can significantly increase your knowledge of a topic.

Towards the end of the book is a section called 'Light Bulb Moments'. This is where you can note down those great ideas that come to you, along with any aha moments. Even if those great ideas don't fit into your plan at the moment, it's useful to look back at them at a later date as they may be appropriate then or they may spark some new ideas.

There are blank spaces in each chapter for you to make notes and write down your thoughts. The more you interact with the workbook, the more buy-in you can have. This is not simply a reading book; this is a way for you to work on your business (and life) and move forward over the year.

Note that this book is for you; our suggestion is that you choose not to show it to anyone else if you prefer not to, which means you can be honest with yourself when writing down your thoughts. The more you are connecting with the 'real you' the more you can work from a place of passion and integrity.

Adopt a system for using the workbook

If you work out a system or habit for using the workbook, for example setting aside a time — or times — each month, you are more likely to make it happen.

What is your system?

____

____

____

____

____

EXERCISE

Begin with the end in mind. Steven Covey

Before you start, look at Chapter 12 — this is where you'll be writing the review of your year. Think through what you could write here in eleven or twelve months' time that would make you feel supremely satisfied with your business journey this year. This will help you complete the chapter on setting goals, and give you an empowering overview of the journey ahead of you.

Accountability

It's very easy to set goals and become fired up about what you are going to achieve over the next twelve months. It's less easy, however, to put in the hard work, deal with the sometimes-mundane tasks required, along with overcoming the challenges that will inevitably crop up on your way to reaching those goals.

Getting the Basics Right

Saying you want to achieve something isn't necessarily the same as *actually* wanting to achieve something, so it's important to set goals you genuinely want to accomplish and are willing to put the work into. You need to establish clear, compelling reasons for your goals that you can call on when the temptation to procrastinate makes an appearance. Once your motivation wanes or becomes unclear, you're more likely to go off track.

One of the reasons you may not complete a task is because you don't know how to do it. When you are setting out your tasks, spend time writing down the step-by-step approach you need to take. If you don't know the steps, the chances are high that those tasks will be left uncompleted. At this point it's important to FIND OUT HOW TO DO THEM. This could very well be the make-or-break point between achieving your goals … or not.

Understand that there are consequences to both action and inaction. For each task you set yourself, note down the outcomes for completion **and** for not getting it done. There **is** an impact for leaving tasks uncompleted.

Accountability

Once you have set your goals in *Chapter 1*, finding a method of accountability that works for you will ensure you keep on track — month after month — as you progress along your business journey.

Accountability strategies include:

Self-accountability

- Set yourself tasks and build in times at defined periods — for example daily or weekly — to evaluate progress and make amendments if needed. Discipline is the name of the game!
- Use an app that helps with accountability and productivity
- Put a visual reminder on display. For example:
  - a calendar which you mark off with a large X when you have completed a task; you'll start to see a row of X's and not want to break it. Check out Jerry Seinfeld's method for creative success online 'Don't Break the Chain'
  - a simple but brightly-coloured note on your desk that says something like "Have you met your targets today?"
  - *lots* of brightly-coloured notes dotted around the place to constantly remind you!
  - reminders that you schedule to pop up on your computer's calendar to encourage (or harass!) you to complete a task
  - a progress chart showing your end goal that you keep filling in as you achieve the next step
  - an inspirational picture or photo (such as your partner or children) that reminds you of your reason for doing what you're doing.

Supported accountability

- Choose a mentor who will help you set appropriate goals and hold you accountable.
- Find a buddy who will work with you on the same — or different — goals, and hold each other accountable. Choose your buddy wisely; you want one who will share tips and strategies with you; who will motivate you and be motivated by you; and who will celebrate the successes you both have along the way.
- Announce your goals to others and ask people to help keep you on track. Once you put it out there you feel more obliged to do it; peer pressure is very helpful; as is actually seeing someone you have told, as they act as a visual reminder for you! You can announce your goals on your blog, Twitter or Facebook, and post regular updates that others can comment on.

Women in Business: Juggling Life's Demands

Are you a busy woman? Do you relate to any of the following?

- You have too many takeaway meals

- You don't see your friends often enough

- Hobbies? Maybe one day

- Your roots are starting to show — must make an appointment at the hairdresser soon

- The amount of unread emails in your inbox is getting a bit scary

- You feel drawn to motivational quotes that say a messy house is a good thing

- You know you have a husband/partner because you've seen the wedding photos, but you really must make some time to see them

How did you do? If you relate to any, or all, or similar issues you are not alone, and you are probably very busy. As a working woman, life places many demands on you. The trick is to manage these demands to ensure you are in control of your activities. Things start to fall apart if you feel the demands are controlling you.

Is there a 'right' way?

In most aspects in life we will fall somewhere on a continuum.

For example, how much 'me time' do you have? Some people fall at one end of the continuum where they don't have any, while others may be at the other end, and have too much. Most people will be somewhere in the middle.

There is no 'right' place to be on the continuum, only a right place for you, given your situation and the needs you are aiming to meet.

My belief is that as we go through life we want to have our needs met. Bear in mind that everyone has individual needs, so what may suit some people may not suit you and your needs. Also remember that your needs change as you go through life.

When we encounter various aspects of life, it's often akin to looking at a beach ball. We may be looking at the same thing as other people, but we are seeing a different angle to it.

For example, if a mother with a young child chooses to take time for her hobby regularly and leave the children with a babysitter, her view may be that it's beneficial, as she is nourishing herself and is therefore better able to parent her children. Someone else's view may be that it's *not* a beneficial situation as the child is losing out on connecting with the mother.

There isn't a 'right' way to look at it, more a right way for you and your situation.

So, when we find ourselves juggling life's demands, there are several issues to consider. Here we'll look a couple of them: What are you juggling, and strategies to deal with the demands.

What are you juggling?

There is a saying which goes 'You can improve what you measure'.

If we don't measure, or have a good understanding of what is taking up our time, it will be hard to make improvements.

What is taking up your time?

First make a list of all the activities you spend your time on.

For example: Work or business; Household chores; Time for marriage; Time with children; Time with other family members and friends; Hobby or recreation; Health and exercise; Quiet time; Watching TV; Community involvement; etc.

Next tick a column *Glass*, *Clay* or *Wool* to show its level of importance, with Glass being the most important and Wool being the least important.

Their level of importance can be determined by what would happen if these activities 'dropped' from your life.

For example, let's say that your husband/partner 'dropped' from your life. How serious would that be? If you feel it would be devastating, then you would label 'time for marriage' as Glass, because it would break if dropped.

If you stopped doing the garden, it became very untidy, and caused you to feel unhappy, then label that as Clay as it goes out of shape if dropped, but can be moulded back to how it was.

If the activity 'watching TV' were removed from your life and you felt it would have no serious or long term effects, then you would label that Wool, as there would be no damage if that activity were dropped, and you can always pick it up again later.

Now write down a rough percentage next to each item as to how much of your time that activity takes up. Make sure they all add up to 100%.

Activity	Glass	Clay	Wool	%
TOTAL %				

Then look at your Glass items. Are you allocating enough time to them?

If not, look at the items labelled Wool. Which of these items can you either remove from your life or spend less time on so that the most important aspects of your life receive the attention they deserve?

If you find yourself juggling too much, the stress is likely to catch up with you sooner or later.

A lecturer, when explaining stress management to an audience, raised a glass of water and asked, "How heavy is this glass of water?"

Answers called out ranged from 20g to 500g.

The lecturer replied, "The absolute weight doesn't matter. It depends on how long you try to hold it.

If I hold it for a minute, that's not a problem.

If I hold it for an hour, I'll have an ache in my right arm.

If hold it for a day, you'll have to call an ambulance.

In each case, it's the same weight, but the longer I hold it, the heavier it becomes."

He continued, "And that's the way it is with stress management. If we carry our burdens all the time, sooner or later, as the burden becomes increasingly heavy, we won't be able to carry on."

Strategies for juggling life's demands

Research has shown that women have two main approaches to juggling life's demands. Firstly, they put into place practical solutions, and secondly they adopt a mental approach or attitude about their situation that works for them.

For example:

Practical techniques

Making the best use of their time

- Working part time and taking longer to build a business
- Living near to work to reduce travelling time
- Reducing out-of-work commitments
- Making a list of all the weekly activities, and delegating those which others can do
- Hiring a cleaner and/or gardener to reduce the tasks they need to perform at home
- Working some evenings and weekends to be able to spend time with children after school
- 'Disconnecting' e.g. not taking the laptop when going away, turning off phone in evenings
- Filling in a diary/calendar and having it on display so all family members can see what needs to be organised
- Preparing as much as possible the night before
- Phoning others on the way home from work to be able to focus on family when home
- Taking a half day or day leave at stress times
- Finding ways to build in exercise for brief free periods of time, e.g. leaving walking shoes or bike at work and going for a brisk walk or cycle ride over lunchtime

Decisions regarding work

- Changing career if the work does not fit in with life values, goals and circumstances
- Role swap with husband/partner who becomes the at-home parent
- Both parents work part time and share childcare between them
- Having a home-based office
- Moving the office out of the home to have a clear delineation

Building in support/respite

- Calling on family members to help
- Working out a system with partner
- Having arrangements with others, for example 'If you take my children to school I will give you free IT support'
- Asking the children to take over some chores
- Arranging childcare to have weekends away on own or with partner
- Self-support: building in me-time, eg massage, meditation, hobby, coffee with friends
- Buying a cheaper house plus a small weekend house and taking regular breaks

Money issues

- Choosing to work part-time and choosing to live more simply
- Bringing in another income, such as taking in a boarder, to reduce the hours worked

Mental approach/attitude

Many women have not only adopted practical techniques, but have also made decisions or adopted mental attitudes that allow them to cope with the demands.

- Looking at work-life balance and seeing that work *is* life. Moving away from the assumption that work is unpleasant, and choosing a business which is in alignment with life values
- Making hours at work non-negotiable — if the hours are too long, find a way to work more efficiently
- Believing that working long hours and having a non-balanced life is OK for a period of time
- Adopting an attitude of 'I'm married to my business and I'm happy this way'
- Setting boundaries so that the situation doesn't control them
- Choosing to move away from the rat race to a quieter, slower pace of life where there are fewer needs and must-dos
- Lowering expectations. For example, having a less tidy house, living in a smaller house, having fewer material possessions, fewer holidays…
- Believing that leaving your child with a nanny or placing them in a childcare centre: is OK … better for them … gives them a better experience … helps them thrive…
- Discussing with their children: 'Do you want me to work more and earn more money, or would you like me to earn less and be able to spend more time with you?'
- Appreciating they can't know the answer to all the issues and choosing to get help, for example from a business coach

If you are working and find yourself juggling many demands, it is possible to take control of the demands rather than allowing the demands to control you. It is possible; it simply requires some thought and some effort.

Write down the first three steps you are going to take:

1 ____

2 ____

3 ____

CHAPTER 1   GOAL SETTING

Stop setting goals. Goals are pure fantasy unless you have a specific plan to achieve them.

Stephen Covey

There are no happier people on this planet than those who decide that they want something, define what they want, get hold of the feeling of it even before its manifestation and then joyously watch the unfolding as, piece by piece by piece, it begins to unfold.

Abraham

A business journey needs to start with clearly defined goals otherwise it just becomes a stroll through a park with a lot of sitting on a bench rather than a big fat, stomach churning, wonderful adventure that leads you to a planned destination.

Begin your fantastic journey by setting effective, achievable goals that will become the heart of your business strategy.

1. **Have very clear, strong reasons** for setting a particular goal and understand what it is you really want to achieve. Goals that are actually achieved are focused around meaningful reasons rather than obvious ones like make more money

2. **What is it you *really* want?** Do you want to increase your income by 30% or do you actually want financial independence to be able to take an overseas trip, upgrade your lifestyle or expand your business?

3. **Take your time**: This is not something to be rushed to fill in a space in your brand new journal. Take the time to think about

    - What you want to achieve in your business and why?

    - What is inspiring you/ driving you to take this journey?

    - What do you need to get there?

4. **Write it down:** Goals that are written down are 10 times more likely to be achieved. This journal is your reference to check in monthly and review — are you on track? Or have you gone towards something shiny that is taking you further away from your business goal? Stay on track, keep focused and see where you have been and what you have achieved

5. **Keep it real and achievable:** What is realistic for you to achieve in the time frame you have set yourself given external factors such as time, family and financial constraints. Set those great big scary goals but make sure that you have a realistic chance of achieving them

6. **Good habits count:** Setting good habits with productivity, time management and planning will help pave the pathway to your goals. What works for you? A daily check-in? Weekly? Best time of day/ week to plan? Don't overload or over think it — keep it simple and regular so it becomes routine and creates good business habits

7. **Are you ready to work for it?** It won't happen because you want it to or because you hope it will, it will only work if you put the work in. Set your big goal, set the smaller goals to achieve that and the set the action plan to achieve them. Small steps towards big changes takes planning, focus and commitment

NOTES

Your own notes on goal setting — for example from a speaker; your own research

BUSINESS GOAL

Where do you want your business to be in 1 year's time?

____

____

Why is that your goal?

____

____

How do you expect it to achieve/impact/change in your life?

____

____

How will it do this?

____

____

____

How will you know you have achieved this?

____

____

Secondary goals to help you achieve your Business Goal

1 ____

2 ____

3 ____

4 ____

PERSONAL GOAL

Why is that your goal?

____

____

What do you expect it to achieve/impact/change in your life?

____

____

How will it do this?

____

____

____

How will you know you have achieved this?

____

____

____

Date achieved

____

Secondary goals to help you achieve your Personal Goal

1 ____

2 ____

3 ____

4 ____

Even the smallest action is better than inaction, so taking it step by step will get you closer to your goal every single day.

5 MINUTE MICRO-ACTIONS

1. Plan a regular 5-minute slot once a week to review your goals for the week ahead. Monday mornings are great for this. Set an appointment on your calendar so you get a reminder
2. Take 5 minutes once a week to look at what you have achieved in the preceding week towards your goals. Seeing what we have already achieved helps the energy to keep going

Monthly Life Areas check-in

Life area	Score out of 10	Notes
Family		
Physical health		
Social/Recreation		
Community		
Learning		
Spiritual		
Personal development		
Other		
Other		

CHAPTER 2　　NETWORKING

It is not about closing sales; it is about opening relationships.

Kevin Knebl

Nothing liberates your greatness like the desire to help, the desire to serve.

Marianne Williamson

The currency of real networking is not greed but generosity.

Keith Ferrazzi

Networking is an effective way to build your business. Joining a business network group, ideally in real life, and also online can bring many rewards. Networking is a much bigger concept than attending a group, but either way, it will only be effective if you understand the principles behind it, and do it well.

1. What is Networking?

A simple definition of networking is that it is the process of meeting people, forming relationships, and developing relationships for the benefit of all parties concerned.

Networking is therefore a 3-step process:

Step 1: Meet people. Both in real life and online. To some degree, networking is a numbers game. If you don't meet many new people, you will have a small network. If you meet a large number people, you can have a much larger network.

Step 2: Form relationships. Spend time talking to people and being genuinely interested in them. Find out about them, not just their work or business but about themselves as a person too.

Step 3: Develop relationships. Aim to develop in-depth relationships. The deeper you can *comfortably* connect with other people, the better network you will have.

Being a good networker takes time and effort. Networking is more akin to farming than hunting — you need to sow the seeds of a business relationship, and cultivate those relationships over time in order to have an effective network. Humans are emotional beings and we prefer to do business with people we like as a human being; we prefer to do business with people we can trust. Effective networking is not about selling, not just working a room, not desperately seeking new business, it's about building connections.

Personality Traits

Networking is a life skill, not something you do when you want something. Great networkers live as networkers and constantly look for ways to connect with others in a way that provides benefit. They focus on others and on what they can give to others. They understand the 'Law of Reciprocity'; that the more you give to others, more will ultimately come back to you. Less successful networkers 'do networking at' people when they want something. They focus on themselves and on what they can get.

Most people describing the qualities of a good networker will focus on their personal characteristics: "They are good listeners" "They remember my name" "They make me feel welcome" "They are interested in people", and so on. The personality traits of a great networker are rated more highly than 'networking techniques'. One of the most important things you can do to become successful at networking is to develop people-focused personality traits that make you likeable and approachable.

They include:

Attitude towards networking

Give without expectation

See connections between people

Have an abundance mentality

Make friends before making requests

Attitude towards others

Believe others are interesting

Make others feel good about themselves

Encourage others to talk about themselves

Personal characteristics

Trustworthy and sincere

Enthusiastic, positive, motivated

Good listeners and communicators

2. Networking Styles

There are many ways to network, and some ways are more effective than others. Let's look at some networking styles:

The Scarcity Networkers

These networkers don't give; they only try to get.

They don't feel there is enough to go around.

They haven't grasped the basic concept of networking, and often try to 'sell'.

They find out little about the other person and may come across as desperate.

The Surface Networkers

These people go to lots of events, meet lots of people, give and receive lots of business cards, but only form 'surface' relationships.

They are often impatient, expecting immediate results and are not in for the long haul.

The Snobbish Networkers

These networkers only want to mix with people of a certain status, not with 'lesser' people. They don't see the benefits that can be reaped from networking with a range of people.

The Social Networkers

These people attend networking events mainly for the social contact. They may or may not be aiming to build their business.

The Selective Networkers

These people know exactly who they want to target.

They narrowcast rather than broadcast, and spend a lot of quality time at it.

They understand that those who give, will reap the rewards.

The Solid Networkers

These networkers are in for the long haul. They understand the concepts of networking, learn the ropes and build long term, lasting relationships.

They do the preparation, they do the work, nurture and cultivate their network, are patient and persevering.

3. Network Regularly

It's what you do on a regular basis that counts. Remember that great networkers live as networkers.

Become known

A large percentage of success is turning up.

- Attend networking events regularly. Become known as the go-to person for your field
- Have a profile in the community. Remember that people in the day to day community could be potential clients or could know people who are your potential clients
- Increase the number of people you come into contact with. Set goals for meeting people — then devise an action plan for how you will do this:

What type of people would you like to meet this month?

____

How many do you want to meet?

____

How can you do this?

____

- Make sure people understand what you do, so they can pass on referrals. How **do** you want to be known? Write your elevator pitch here — a short description of what you do and the benefits your product or service provides — that you could say in less than a minute:

____

____

____

Keep in touch

- Maintain your database and make contact regularly — at a minimum four times a year, ideally more

- Give! Great networkers are great givers

    - Give referrals/promote others
    - Give your time to help others, for example to connect people for *their* mutual benefit; to pass on useful information or invitations
    - Give things of value for free (choose wisely what you give)
    - Give thank you's and testimonials in person and in public

Prepare for a network event

The more you prepare for an event, the more you are likely to benefit from it and be able to provide benefit to others.

Purpose

Determine your purpose(s) before you go to the event. It may be something simple, such as to meet one new person and form a contact in another organisation. If you have a purpose, it makes it easier to talk to people.

Mental preparation

Many people are nervous before going to an event. To help reduce nerves:

- Prepare some questions to ask; situational ones such as "Have you been to one of these events before?" and business ones such as "Who is your ideal client? I may already know someone."

- Be prepared to come out of your comfort zone, not stay with people you know

- Choose a frame of mind where you 'act like the host not the guest'. This gives you a greater sense of belonging, and therefore a greater feeling of confidence

- Practise your elevator pitch so you can answer the question "What do you do?"

- Think of what — or how — you might be able to give

Practical Preparation

Make sure you choose the most appropriate clothing for the occasion.

Know what times the event starts; if you need to pay; how to get to there; where to park and so on, so you arrive feeling as calm and as well prepared as you can.

Take your business cards. Take enough, in good condition, with accurate contact details.

Take flyers or items to give out or display.

When at a networking event

When talking with someone, give them your undivided attention; don't look over their shoulder to see if someone more interesting has arrived!

Stand, don't sit. Once you sit, it's harder to mix with people.

Don't stay with colleagues. It's fine to have a chat with them for a few minutes, but don't stay with them all the time.

If it's a longer event, such as a conference, try sitting with different people during the event.

Getting to speak to people

If you feel nervous, remember that most people probably feel the same way. They may not look it — people generally don't — but then neither will you. To make things easier, go early. It gives you more networking time, and it's easier to talk to people as they come in, rather than walking into a crowded room. Approach people who come alone. Few people like to stand on their own, and they will appreciate someone talking to them.

How to break into groups

Look friendly — smile, smile, smile! People like people who smile.

Try watching what happens with groups: how they form, how long they stay together, how they separate. One thing you'll notice after a while is that some groups look like they want people to come into them (open groups), and some groups don't (closed groups). The group that has open body language — they are not in a complete circle, have a gap or space, or somebody's eyes are distracted and are looking away — are saying they are happy for someone to come in and join the group.

How to get away

The informal guidelines around networking events are that you talk to someone for approximately 3–8 minutes and then move on, so don't feel that you will be offending someone if you move away. Bring it to a natural conclusion, for example say "It's been nice talking to you" and ask for their business card; or make it a benefit to them by you leaving, "I know you have a number of people to speak to, so I won't hold you up any longer."

You can suggest you go to the coffee/food area, as it's easier to 'swap partners' around food and drink.

After the Event

Write something on their business card so you can remember them.

Follow up on promises, for example give the phone number you promised to provide.

Contact those you have an affinity with.

Building a network can be rewarding and fun. Great networkers understand the fundamental principles and build strong networks that can bring them many benefits.

5 MINUTE MICRO-ACTIONS

- After each network event, spend 5 minutes contacting someone you have a synergy with and arrange, for example, to meet them for coffee
- Once a week write a testimonial for a contact on LinkedIn. Great networkers have a mentality of giving, so by giving positive reinforcement to others, it builds stronger networking relationships

NOTES

Your own notes on Networking — for example from a speaker; your own research

ANALYSIS

How would you rate yourself as a networker? What do you do well? What could you improve?

GOALS

Set yourself some realistic networking goals

Goal	Timeframe	Accountability method

RESULTS

My outcomes

NEXT STEP

Monthly Life Areas check-in

Life area	Score out of 10	Notes
Family		
Physical health		
Social/Recreation		
Community		
Learning		
Spiritual		
Personal development		
Other		
Other		

CHAPTER 3   SOCIAL MEDIA

Being effective at social media, whether for business or personal use, means capturing people who have short attention spans. They're only a click away from a picture of a funny cat, so you have to make your thing more compelling than that cat. And that can be a high bar.

Alexis Ohanian

There's a danger in the internet and social media. The notion that information is enough, that more and more information is enough, that you don't have to think, you just have to get more information — gets very dangerous.

Edward de Bono

Social media is the ultimate equalizer. It gives a voice and a platform to anyone willing to engage. It is changing the way we communicate and the way we are perceived, both positively and negatively. Every time you post a photo, or update your status, you are contributing to your own digital footprint and personal brand.

Amy Jo Martin

Over the period of a few years, social media has hugely impacted and disrupted the way many people do business. Customers have become more accessible and your ability to engage and interact with them directly has risen significantly.

Instead of selling we're connecting, instead of large expensive print campaigns we run small targeted online campaigns with little outlay that can be stopped or boosted at a push of a button, and connects us instantly with our target audience.

You may be a small business operating out of your spare room, juggling family, life and growing a business, but online you can project a very different image. You can be a professional, an industry leader, the owner of a global business. You can be the business you want to be perceived as online.

The lack of physical boundaries in social media means that businesses now have the potential to connect to customers anywhere in the world. If you can ship, post or Skype you can do business there. The downside of this is that your competition increases too. You're no longer competing with just the businesses in your neighbourhood, anyone can access your customers.

Social media has created a new level of accountability with businesses needing to lift their customer service (which can't be a bad thing), as angry and unhappy customers can now share their negative experience with, quite literally, everyone. For small businesses with excellent customer service this can be a huge benefit, and levels the playing field with larger less customer-focused companies.

It can feel like a constant whirl of holiday snaps and cat videos but social media has become our information source, our connection, our place to tell, read and be part of stories. If social media does not have a place in your business strategy maybe you need to reconsider that.

Make it right for YOU

Understanding that you need social media is not enough. There is constant hype and talk — post here, tweet there, snap this, create that. Cut through the overwhelm and decide what's right for YOUR business.

Whether you are stepping out into the social media world for the first time or need to re-evaluate your current social media activity, take the time now to **really** think about what you want your social media activity to achieve for you and your business.

Social media strategy

Use these next steps to form the basis of your social media strategy for the year ahead.

As part of your strategy you need to have 3 things:

1. Intent

Don't be on social media for the sake of it. Know why you are using social media, what do you want to get out of it? If you are not using it with purpose the you are frankly wasting your time. If you are half hearted it shows, which counters any good impressions you might otherwise be building.

Having 1000+ contacts on Facebook has no value unless

- They are your target market
- You have a plan to get them to take action i.e. buy/join/engage your services

What is your purpose for using social media? What do you want it to do for your business? For example, buy more, become customers, understand your services better

____

____

What platforms are your clients/potential customers using?

____

____

2. Understanding

How and why are your potential clients using social media? For example, they might be on Facebook but are they just there to post pictures and chat with their friends or are they using it as a news/ information resource? Are they in online groups — which ones and why? Do they use Instagram or Pinterest to build a "dream life"? Do your research:

- look at current customers, see what they are doing
- find out what platforms your target demographic is using
- see what your competition is doing and how that is working

How are your clients/ potential customers using social media?

____

____

____

Why are your clients/ potential customers using social media?

____

____

What platforms are they using?

____

____

3. Commitment

Building a social media strategy takes time and commitment. Random posting on Facebook a few times a week doesn't cut it. Social Media is not free; it costs you time away from your business and can be a huge time suck so you have to ensure the time spent = more business. To do this you need a strategy you can stick to and the commitment to follow through for a set period of time.

Platforms

Facebook

With more than 1 billion people using Facebook daily it is still the number one social media choice for most businesses. It's an online platform where you can sell or promote a product/service to a highly targeted audience and is very much focused on connecting, engaging and sharing. Complicated algorithms as well as the sheer volume of activity can make it challenging to consistently reach your market without a clear strategy, and concentrated effort. There are tools such as buffer.com to help with this as well as Facebook advertising as an option.

Facebook groups have grown significantly and are a great place for service industries to build their audience and reputation by being helpful, generous, relevant and knowledgeable in a personal, non-threatening way.

Twitter

Being confined to 140 characters forces businesses to get their messages out in the clearest, most concise manner possible. It's also great for brand awareness so think about your Twitter persona — be approachable, active and professional. Twitter is perhaps the best platform to connect with industry leaders, influencers and media. While there is definite etiquette around this, they are accessible and approachable on Twitter like no other platform. Twitter provides great resource which can be excellent for learning and sharing but can also be a huge time suck so use well and with caution.

LinkedIn

A professional networking site, primarily for connecting with other professionals but is also the perfect platform for posting well-written and researched blogs and articles. It's the place other professionals check out your qualifications, credentials and past experience.

YouTube

Is surprisingly the second largest online search engine and widely used as a resource for how-to content. What questions do you get asked a lot? Make a short video taking them through the solution/process. It's a great place and opportunity to share your knowledge and show your personality. YouTube videos can be embedded on your site and shared through other platforms.

Pinterest

Image-based Pinterest has been a significant driver of traffic for product based businesses for a while but has this year been noted as a serious component in any social media strategy. Bloggers and service based businesses have been capitalising on this platform using images, inspirational posts and infographics in their articles and websites that are getting pinned around the world and providing roads back to their businesses. Beware of locality settings — there is no point having lots of pins and traffic from people that will never be your customers.

Instagram

Originally used by young selfie-takers, looking at dream lives, Instagram has now grown its demographic with 400 million users globally. This is a highly engaged and active community that is the go to place for building and showcasing your brand through images, short videos clips, and cohesive visual content. A platform that takes thought and preparation to decide on the overall aesthetic you are projecting. Do your research, look at similar industries, post with care.

5 steps to Your Social Media Strategy

1. Define social media goals

2. Choose which platform(s)

3. Allocate regular realistic time

4. Create a content plan (what content and when)

5. Plan how and when will you measure your return

Social Media constantly changes

Always stay up to date with what your target market is doing on social media. What works now might not work next year or in a different location. For example, a business who had used Facebook successfully to drive website sales in New Zealand, found this didn't work when they expanded into Australia. After some research they found Australians in their demographic of 30–55yr olds, preferred Instagram which they switched their social media efforts to and found an immediate increase in sales with this one change. This is why you keep measuring and checking your social media return.

5 MINUTE MICRO-ACTIONS

- Take 5 minutes to subscribe to some online social media market sites such as www. socialmediaexaminer.com/ or www.hootsuite.com for regular tools and tips
- Search *Social Media Strategy Templates* and find the one that suits you — there are heaps to choose from.

NOTES

Your own notes on Social Media — for example from a speaker; your own research

ANALYSIS

How would you rate yourself regarding social media? What do you do well? What could you improve?

GOALS

Set yourself some realistic social media goals

Goal	Timeframe	Accountability method

RESULTS

My outcomes

NEXT STEP

Monthly Life Areas check-in

Life area	Score out of 10	Notes
Family		
Physical health		
Social/Recreation		
Community		
Learning		
Spiritual		
Personal development		
Other		
Other		

CHAPTER 4   MARKETING 1

Target Market; Value Proposition

The aim of marketing is to know and understand the customer so well the product or service fits him and sells itself.

Peter Drucker

In marketing I've seen only one strategy that can't miss — and that is to market to your best customers first, your best prospects second and the rest of the world last.

John Romero

Marketing drives your business. It builds connections with prospective customers interested in what your business offers and clearly shows the value in a way that is easily understood and creates the need to purchase.

To be able to market effectively you need to understand 2 core aspects:

1. Who your market is

2. Why they should buy from you

Who is your market?

If you don't know the answer to this question (and no, it is not 'everyone'), your marketing effort could be a complete waste of time and money. You need to know **who** you are talking/connecting to if you want your marketing to be effective.

Look at your existing customers to identify similarities between your regular customers so you can begin to use this information to refine your existing customer base into a target market.

- Why do your existing customers choose your business over your competitors?
- What are their common characteristics?
- What are their common interests?

When researching target markets, start wide and narrow it down as much as possible. For example, you may identify homeowners as a potential demographic BUT when you drill down deeper you discover that homeowners with older children, earning a certain annual income who work in a particular sector are your best customers.

This level of segmentation makes it easier to create specific marketing to appeal to those individuals rather than a general customer base, i.e. better conversion to sales. Use these demographics to help you define your target market by painting a picture of your customer — where are they, who are they, what are their interests and values, and what is their buying behaviour?

Geographic: Location

Demographic: Gender, Age, Household size, Marital status, Occupation, Education, Language spoken, Children, Age of children

Psychographic: Personality, Values, Attitude, Interests, Lifestyle

Behavioural: Products/services purchased, Channels used to purchase, Rate of usage, Why bought, How used.

The more defined your market is the more detailed and focused your marketing can be; *for example,* Wellington women 30yrs+, running their own business from home for a flexible lifestyle, looking to connect, learn and grow their business.

Who is your Target Market?
Be as detailed as possible

____

____

____

What is your Value Proposition? i.e. Why should they buy from you?

Your value proposition is a clear statement about the actual benefits customers obtain from using your product or service. When you have established this, it should be used in your emails, marketing and presentations to help potential customers quickly and easily understand why they should buy or engage your services.

To create a strong, clear value proposition, you need to know:

What problem are you solving? Where is their pain, what are they struggling with?

What is the purpose of what you sell? What does it do, what are the features?

What are the benefits of your product/service? Customers don't buy products and services — they buy the benefits the products and services provide for them; they want solutions.

Example 1

Problem: a large family in a small house with an unsafe outdoor area

Feature: a building company that can build a deck for extended living and manage the whole project from start to finish

Benefit: a safe, usable space built quickly and professionally to your specifications without you having to deal with the details or take time away from your job or family, that also increases the resale value of your home

Example2

Problem: Out of date website losing sales and incurring costs to have any small changes made

Feature: fresh new website that you can manage yourself and make changes any time

Benefit: saving of time and money (not needing a developer) and (with fresh new business focus site) converting more customers

When you understand the benefit of your product/service, your marketing can clearly show them **WHY** they should buy.

Does your product/service reduce stress, save time, save money, give people energy, increase wellbeing?

Adding "so you can" makes you think about what the benefit actually is that will make the customer purchase.

Here is a useful formula to describe your benefits:

Your product/service + primary feature "so you can" describe the benefit it brings the customer.

Use the formula above and describe your benefits

____

____

____

Why purchase from you?

Now we understand the benefits, but why should people purchase from you and not someone else? Are there similar products/services on the market?

What makes yours special/better/different? **What is your unique selling point/competitive advantage?**

For example, your values, your services, presentation, tagline etc. Find something to be memorable.

*"In order to be remembered in a crowded marketplace, it helps if your business has a trait that is **worth remembering**."* Theodore Levitt, author and professor at Harvard Business School

Do your research. Check out your competition and see what you do better. Ask existing customers why they chose you. If you don't know why you are better than your competition or why people buy from you, how will potential customers know?

List why your customers should choose you:

____

____

____

____

5 MINUTE MICRO-ACTIONS

- Start grouping your clients into demographics to help you track and determine your actual target market. Use a CRM or spreadsheet whatever keeps it easy for you to maintain
- Write a short survey to existing or previous clients to see where they found the benefit of your product or service

NOTES

Your own notes on Marketing — for example from a speaker; your own research

ANALYSIS

How would you rate yourself regarding marketing — your target market and why they should buy from you?

What do you do well? What could you improve?

GOALS

Set yourself some realistic marketing goals

Goal	Timeframe	Accountability method

RESULTS

My outcomes

NEXT STEP

My outcomes

Monthly Life Areas check-in

Life area	Score out of 10	Notes
Family		
Physical health		
Social/Recreation		
Community		
Learning		
Spiritual		
Personal development		
Other		
Other		

CHAPTER 5   MARKETING 2

Marketing Strategy

People are in such a hurry to launch their product or business that they seldom look at marketing from a bird's eye view and they don't create a systematic plan.

Dave Ramsey

Word-of-mouth marketing is a crucial component of organic growth for start-ups and one of the primary ways that our company has grown to over 15 million customers.

David Rusenko

A Marketing Strategy helps you focus on your business goals and decide on the best way to talk to your customers (which marketing channels) in a clearly defined way that can be easily developed into an effective *marketing plan* that is well thought out and effective.

Building your Marketing Strategy

1. Set your goals and objectives
2. Work out your budget
3. Clearly define who you are targeting
4. Decide on your marketing channels
5. Put this all together in an actionable marketing plan

Set your goals and objectives

If you don't know where you're going, how do you know when you get there?

- What results do you want to achieve with your marketing?
- What's the primary reason for marketing?

Marketing goals should fit into and support your overall business goals and be measurable.

- Get X new customers by Y
- Launch a new product or product-line by X
- Increase website traffic by X
- Grow revenue X% by Y

Work out your budget

Know what a customer is worth to you, to help you determine what to spend. This will also help determine which channels to use. If a customer is worth $100 to you, then spending $10 to get one customer is OK, but if your customer is worth only $20, not so much …

Clearly define who you are targeting

Decide who your target market is for each campaign and make it as detailed as possible for the best results i.e. high conversion.

Which marketing channels?

Referral: People purchasing products or services based on someone else's opinion or influence. A primary source of business for many service industries, referral marketing is deliberately encouraging your customers to talk about you. This can be done with requests for reviews, feedback, testimonials; it is earned via great service, doing your job well and being generous and memorable. It's the easiest and cheapest marketing, and one of the most effective as it comes from a trusted independent source.

Repeat business: For most small businesses, acquiring new customers is the **least** efficient way to generate sales. The **most** efficient way is through your existing customers. They understand the value and have already given you money for it. If you have had good sales but for one-off products or services, what add-on or extra services could you offer? You have a waiting client base.

Networking: While networking can be one of the most cost effective channels of marketing, it can be time consuming and is not for short term returns. It needs an investment of time to have intent and to have a follow up process. Excellent again for service industries where referral and word of mouth is your main source of business as you can get to know a lot of people in a short amount of time. Refer to the Networking chapter for the "how to".

PR: Obtaining free PR is easier than you might think — it involves pitching a story rather than a sales pitch, but has good uptake and credibility because of not being perceived as an advertisement. This generally only works if your market is local. Other options are paid and you should make sure you look at the metrics and potential return on investment before committing. There are PR companies that can also help you navigate these waters.

Promotional Material: You always need a business card; it shows you back yourself and you're serious about your business. Flyers are great for giving more information but are better handed out to interested people that dropped randomly into letter boxes. All promotional material needs to be used with intent rather than hoping that they find an interested person. Banner, poster and other collateral — the same principle applies — what is your intent and expectation, and are they being seen by your target market?

Guerrilla Marketing: Generally low-cost, unconventional marketing tactics that grab attention and are memorable. A fun and interesting marketing channel where execution is key. Tied in with social media it can be very effective and reach a wide audience very quickly.

Web content & SEO: Your website is not just about providing information, it's where your potential customers make their buying decisions, so you want to make this as clear and easy as you can. Each page should have a purpose and take them one step closer to a purchase. Remember the website is for them, not you, and content should clearly show your benefits and value prop throughout. Optimising for SEO is important for being found online for your keywords, which should be used throughout your content. There are several online keyword tools you can use to identify your primary keywords.

Direct Mail: Still very effective with the right messages and a follow up process. Always know who you are talking to and do it with intent and purpose. Spamming is not tolerated and harms your reputation. Again, it's about them so don't bombard people with everything about you; position your emails to always provide value. Individual, personal emails for service-based businesses convert the best, but for larger group emails there are platforms such as MailChimp that can help.

TV and Radio: can be expensive, so you would want to be sure of your ROI. This has diminished significantly for some industries in recent years. Social media has changed the landscape of this more traditional marketing, and it has made it more affordable — do your research and find a way to test before you invest too much.

Workshops: Great for service industries to share knowledge and build a reputation by showcasing your expertise. It is often more time consuming than anticipated so be prepared, and ensure it's aimed at your market. Focus on giving value and having a good follow up process in place to convert participants to engaged clients.

Marketing Action Plan

Clear consistent messages across all channels

Use your benefits and unique selling points to develop key messages for your marketing. Keep this consistent across all channels including social media.

Create a clear pathway to conversion

All your marketing needs a clear call to action, otherwise it's just information. If you are handing out flyers — what do you want people to do? Call? Email? Go to your website?

If you are marketing online to entice people to your website, what do you want them to do when they get there? Make it clear and easy for them to buy/contact/engage.

Measure, Measure, Measure

What is your call to action — phone call, email or visits to website? Record how many times this takes place within the period of your campaign. From this, record how many people convert e.g. traffic to website (X) number of sales (Y). Total sales value (Z)

Use this simple template for each marketing campaign

Campaign Goals	
Campaign Budget	
Target Market	
Key Messages	
Calls to Action	

Channels	Expected Outcome	Actual Outcome	Review

5 MINUTE MICRO-ACTIONS

- Work out the actual value of a customer to you (Average Value of a Sale) x (Number of Repeat Transactions) x (Average Retention Time in Months or Years for a Typical Customer) eg. $20 x 12 months x 3 years = $720 in total revenue (or $240 per year)
- Work out the CAC — Cost of Acquiring a Customer (current marketing expenses) DIVIDED by (the number of new customers you acquire)
  - Facebook advertising spend $100, obtain 2 customers CAC= $50
  - Flyer advertising spend $400, obtain 20 customers CAC= $20

NOTES

Your own notes on Marketing — for example from a speaker; your own research.

NOTES

  © Kim Chamberlain and Iona Elwood-Smith

ANALYSIS

How would you rate yourself regarding your marketing strategy?

What do you do well? What could you improve?

GOALS

Set yourself some realistic marketing goals

Goal	Timeframe	Accountability method

GOALS

Set yourself some realistic marketing goals

RESULTS

My outcomes

NEXT STEP

Monthly Life Areas check-in

Life area	Score out of 10	Notes
Family		
Physical health		
Social/Recreation		
Community		
Learning		
Spiritual		
Personal development		
Other		
Other		

CHAPTER 6   THE SALES PROCESS

It's about caring enough to create value for customers. If you get that part right, selling is easy.

S. Anthony Iannarino

By far the best way to influence people is to start by really listening to them.

Charles H Green

Prospects equal options. Master prospecting and you will be the master of your sales destiny.

Tibor Shanto

Call the leads that fell through the cracks. There's never a reason to let a lead pass you by.

Kendra Lee

Despite the huge change in the way we do business that has taken place over the last decade, there is still a lot of stigma and resistance around sales. People don't like to think of themselves as salespeople or appear pushy. Yes, the car salesman stereotype is alive and well! However, if you have done your research on the client and what they need, you are offering a solution to their problem and providing value. They need what you have, and it's up to you to let them know that.

Marketing is now playing a much larger part in the sales process by generating more qualified leads that come directly to you via your website, social media, online marketing, and so on, which means the sales role has shifted significantly to one of engagement and customer service.

The role of the sales person today is to cut through the overwhelm for the client, helping them understand benefits and value, but most importantly clearly defining what they need to do next. Sales is still relationship-building and following up, which many businesses are neglecting in this new, faster-paced internet world. This is an opportunity for the people who do it well to significantly stand out from their competition.

You may have more people coming to you directly through your marketing, but without a sales process all you actually have is traffic and not conversion.

Lead Generation

Your marketing is doing its job and sending traffic to your website — now what? How do you get people to take action?

1. Key messages on your website highlighting the benefits and value of your service

2. Strong calls to action

This is great for people who are ready to take that step, but what if they are not quite ready yet? They need to think more, talk to someone; they may not be sure if they *really* need what you offer ... so they may wander off and look at their Facebook page or check out another site. How do you get them to contact YOU?

Offer them something of value — a giveaway; a checklist; the top ten things to xxx; or an e-book for example, in return for their email address. You now have their contact details in order to start an interaction with them, and put a lead-generation sales process in place.

There are many tools you can use to set this up via downloads on your website, for example privy.com SumoMe.com, both of which have free versions.

How to be a Good Salesperson

1. Look from the customer's perspective

2. **Listen**; they will tell you what they need and why

3. Understand and be able to clearly articulate the benefit and value of your product or service

4. Talk normally as if you were speaking to a friend, no need to go into 'sales' mode

5. Keep it all about them

6. Provide a clear pathway for what they need to do next

7. Invite action — email, meeting, purchase

8. Follow up, follow up, follow up

When you build a relationship and understand what your customers want, you'll find they trust you and want to do business with you.

The Sales Process

To get more sales and grow their business many people think they need better or more marketing. "If more people knew about me I would get more business." More often it is the sales process of converting those that are already coming, that is the biggest issue. Carrying out additional marketing when this is the problem just means you are sending more people to a leaky funnel.

Solution: Tighten up your sales processes and increase your conversion rate.

Why Do You Need a Sales Process?

You get an inquiry through your website, what do you do? Most people email reply with the information and perhaps a quote or proposal. OK then what? For most people, nothing. "They didn't email back". Um OK … that's actually your job … you want the sale, right? Statistically you get more sales conversion on the second email or even the third. Follow up and ask if they want more information, if you can help any way etc. etc. What you are looking for is engagement — even if they genuinely don't want to buy right now you want (need) to know why. Some sales can happen a year later, though not if you don't stay in touch or appear on their radar.

For every contact or interaction you have with a potential client you need a sales process to ensure everyone is followed up with and you don't drop the ball. I highly recommend using a CRM (customer relationship management) such as capsulecrm.com to manage this, as it can be very hard to remember who to contact when — which is how customer and sales slip by.

Sales Processes

Networking

1. Meet (contact)
2. Conversation (qualify, don't pre-judge)
3. Follow Up (email offering something useful — link info)
4. Send update on anything relevant that might be interesting
5. Suggest meeting if interest established
6. Meet
7. Send proposal
8. If not engaged continue regular interaction with anything that might be helpful to their business with regular calls to action and special offers

Online through website

1. Is prequalified — already expressing interest
2. Email within 24 hours to answer questions and arrange a meeting
3. Meet
4. Send proposal
5. If not engaged continue regular interaction with anything that might be helpful to their business with regular calls to action and special offers

Lead Generation

1. They have downloaded your 'lead magnet'
2. Automated email after download
3. *Email within 5 days with interesting relevant information
4. *Email within 8 days with further information relevant to your product
5. *Email within 2 weeks with special offer and call to action
6. *If not engaged, continue regular interaction (newsletter) with anything that might be helpful

* These emails can be automated through an email service such as MailChimp

Market stall

1. Set up a competition or offer free sample for email addresses
2. Email within 2 days with interesting relevant information
3. Email within a week with further information relevant to your product
4. Email within 2 weeks with special offer and call to action
5. If not engaged continue regular interaction (newsletter) with anything that might be helpful

Existing clients

1. Send regular information/updates that may be useful to them
2. What other services/products can be offered?
3. Can they refer anyone?

Most people do not follow up, yet it is the Number One easiest thing to do to get more sales. Making this change will increase your conversion, show the quality of your service, and make you memorable in the eyes of your potential customers.

5 MINUTE MICRO-ACTIONS

- Take 5 minutes a day every day this week to write out your sales process for each kind of customer interaction you might encounter
- Check back through your emails and see how many you have not followed up with

NOTES

Your own notes on The Sales Process — for example from a speaker; your own research

ANALYSIS

How would you rate yourself regarding The Sales Process? What do you do well? What could you improve?

GOALS

Set yourself some realistic sales process goals

Goal	Timeframe	Accountability method

RESULTS

My outcomes

NEXT STEP

Monthly Life Areas check-in

Life area	Score out of 10	Notes
Family		
Physical health		
Social/Recreation		
Community		
Learning		
Spiritual		
Personal development		
Other		
Other		

CHAPTER 7   INSPIRATION

I long to speak out the intense inspiration that comes to me from the lives of strong women.

Ruth Benedict

I don't get my inspiration from books or a painting. I get it from the women I meet.

Carolina Herrera

I've always looked to other women for inspiration and kicks. When a woman stands up and does her thing, it never ceases to excite and inspire me.

Neneh Cherry

Benefits of Inspiration

As you travel happily along your business journey, you sometimes realise that maybe it's not *always* that happy, it's sometimes, well, a bit ordinary or even a challenge. You get caught up in the day to day activities of running a business, and may not always feel motivated or inspired.

Therefore, it's useful to value the importance of inspiration and take steps to allow more of it to come into your life. Why? Because it's hard to achieve success if you are uninspired; and because feeling inspired brings many benefits:

- The higher your level of inspiration, the higher your level of productivity. When you are feeling inspired you are more likely to achieve your goals with less effort and fewer breaks in the proceedings
- Inspiration helps with creativity, which can help you solve problems more easily, and reach your goal more quickly
- It can move you from indifference to being more aware of potential
- It changes how you view what you are capable of. You may realise you are capable of so much more than you originally thought
- It increases your feelings of well-being, enhancing your sense of purpose and making you more grateful for what you have and what you are now able to do

Aspects of Inspiration

Studies show that there are three aspects to inspiration. Firstly, that it just happens, it isn't something you can force. Secondly that it raises you higher than your usual way of being, mentally taking you beyond your perceived limits and giving you an awareness of other, better ways. And thirdly it involves carrying out a new idea, action or behaviour.

Sadly, our society fosters a high level of evaluation; we are judged for example during exams, when we start a new role, when we meet the potential in-laws, and so on. We may seek to gain approval from people in many ways, even if we don't realise it, and even if people don't realise they are evaluating us. Note that if you are always trying to prove yourself and always trying to please others, you will have less time to be who you really are and less time to be inspired, to try out new things and to take risks. Fear of judgment will lead you to staying in a safe, known comfort zone.

However, if you move past the need to prove yourself, and open yourself to inspiration, take a new idea, work it and mould it, it can produce life-enhancing effects for you.

It may, in addition, produce beneficial flow-on effects for others.

Note that there are differences when it comes to being inspired. If people were placed on a continuum for how easily inspired they were, some would fall at the Easily Inspired end, some wold fall at the Rarely Inspired end, and most people would be dotted along the continuum.

Those at the Easily Inspired end tend to be those who:

- Are open to new experiences
- Want to do their work well
- Are less competitive
- Are intrinsically, not extrinsically, motivated
- Are more likely to achieve goals
- Are more likely to set inspired goals

How to Increase the Likelihood of Being Inspired

Firstly, don't *try* to be inspired; it's not something you can force yourself to do. You don't need to put in effort, but you will have more chance of success if you create the optimal circumstances for allowing inspiration to happen.

There is a formula which goes: *Preparation + Opportunity = Success*

Prepare yourself to be inspired so that when the opportunity arises, you can successfully reap the most reward from it:

- Have an 'openness to experience' — be open to having new experiences, new ways of thinking, new ways of seeing things. The more open you are to experiences, the more you'll be able to recognise inspiration when it's present. Not everyone does
- Make time to do something creative; learn something new; do something different — come out of your regular routine
- Celebrate small achievements; they are important to boosting inspiration
- Have a way to record your ideas as soon as you get them — a notepad or app for example; once they go out of your head it may be hard to retrieve them. Use the 'Light Bulb Moments' section near the end of this book.

Ways to Find Inspiration

There are many ways to find inspiration, and people are inspired differently. You may be enormously inspired by something that has no effect at all on another person. That's OK, you need to be open to inspiration in a range of ways and find what works for you. Examples include:

- Attending business network meetings
- Reading inspirational stories, articles or books
- Going to an event to listen to a speaker
- Choosing to be around inspirational people
- Writing a journal
- Keeping inspirational quotes, looking at them from time to time, choosing one that speaks to you and taking some action
- Watching an online video, for example TED talks
- Doing a mind map or having a discussion with someone about possibilities

- Taking a step forward and doing something you didn't feel you could do
- Bringing peace into your life to allow yourself to become grounded and open to experiences — take a walk in nature; drive through the countryside; go on a short holiday in beautiful natural surroundings

Note down other ways that work for you:

____

____

____

____

Think of times when you have been inspired. Choose your 'best' one.

What inspired you?

____

____

____

Why?

____

____

____

What were you inspired to do?

____

____

____

What were the benefits?

____

____

____

Is there a way this can help you going forward?

____

____

____

Inspiring Others

Remember that the more we give, the more we gain. Each of us can benefit from inspiration from others.

How do you think you have inspired others?

____

____

____

What have been the benefits?

____

____

____

The more you become the best version of you, the more you can inspire others. How can you continue to inspire people? There are many ways, including:

- Doing what you love, doing it well, and doing it with passion and enthusiasm
- Finding the positive in others and letting them know
- Sharing your story with those following the same path as you; explaining your challenges and how you overcame them; sharing your successes
- Believing that there is enough to go around and so being willing to share knowledge, information and referrals that are of help to others
- Taking an interest in others; seeing what they are capable of and challenging and supporting them to do their best
- Showing an appropriate level of vulnerability; letting people know you get things wrong; showing them you can pick yourself up and carry on

Note down other ways that work for you:

____

____

____

5 MINUTE MICRO-ACTIONS

- Watch a 5-minute TED talk
- Listen to an inspirational song
- Do some exercise and get the blood pumping
- Disconnect from technology; give yourself time out to relax and clear your mind
- Who do you admire and find inspirational? Make contact and see if you can meet with them

GOALS

Set yourself some realistic inspiration goals

Goal	Timeframe	Accountability method

RESULTS

My outcomes

NEXT STEP

NOTES

Your own notes on Inspiration — for example from a speaker; your own research

ANALYSIS

How easily inspired are you? Do you have an openness to experience that fosters inspiration? What inspirational situations do you put yourself in? What could you improve?

INSPIRATIONAL STORIES

The single thing all women need in the world is inspiration, and inspiration comes from storytelling.
Zainab Salbi

150 Fax Machines

Sandy Geyer

It is April 1996 and I am in my office in Cape Town with a panoramic view of Table Mountain. A heavily pregnant corporate sales executive I am on the phone to a client I have been visiting for over two years with no returns. Today he wants to know if he can order 150 fax machines. I say, "I will call you right back" and go bounding up the office stairs, two at a time, seven month pregnancy as forgotten as the sight of my toes, to burst rudely into my boss's office with my request. He dials Johannesburg immediately. A flurry of activity ensues and it appears there are 165 fax machines in stock on the system. Yes, head office say, you can have 150 fax machines and WELL DONE!

"The faxes just disappeared off the system," my boss says quietly when I am back in his office later that day with the last of the paperwork for his signature. "A tender from Zimbabwe came in shortly after your order and they had to make a call. The Zimbabwe tender won. I am sorry". I am back in my office. I pick up the phone to my husband. "I am starting my own business," I say.

"You are what?" my husband is shocked. "But don't something like 90% of all new businesses fail?" He continues to reason with me frantically until I promise him I will reconsider. I have no intention whatsoever of reconsidering.

Eighteen months into the new business our accountant tells us that on paper we are bankrupt. We change accountants. It takes us six years to break even and eight years to become profitable.

Eighteen years on and I have the privilege of leading four successful entities across three countries. I have come to understand that whilst security remains an illusion in any profession, *choice* is a real life incentive. I get to choose when and where I work, and with whom. And I get to choose where my family live.

I also get to choose where the 150-fax machines go.

Being an entrepreneur is not a comfortable place to be. During our formative years I was in a constant state of anxiety. There seemed to be more wrong than right much of the time and having staggered to the top of one mountain, another far more daunting one appeared. Trusted staff stole from us, loyal clients abandoned us and political influences undermined us. Moving from barely surviving to courageously pioneering was simply about getting good at what we did as quickly as possible. We had to take complete charge of our challenges along the way to do that.

It is our entrepreneurial abilities that will determine the future stability of our economies. Our evolving world needs us, but to be successful in entrepreneurship we have to be ready to reveal all that we are capable of, ready or not. And whilst we are all capable- we are never ready. Something just needs to matter that much to us. It is in how deeply that something matters that we discover, and are driven to sharpen the traits needed to push us through.

Losing the 150 fax machines mattered that much to me and I am eternally grateful to the universe for taking them.

Sandy Geyer founded Allcopy Publishers in 1996, Quickvest Properties in 2003, Mind Action Mentors in 2008 and EnQPractice in 2012. She travels between South Africa, Australia and New Zealand inspiring and empowering entrepreneurs to develop their Entrepreneurial Intelligence (EnQ) and take control of their destinies. www.enqpractice.com

Don't Give Negative Thoughts Any Airplay

Leanne Babcock

My vision was to help people and make a difference in the world while at the same time being able to earn an income, and the job I was doing back in 1993 didn't allow me to do that. So I mind-mapped what I needed to do. It was very basic, I had no business plan, I simply wrote down what I thought I could offer — types of coaching and training — based on what I was experienced in and what I knew worked. I also wrote down what my target income was for the first year — $100,000.

I understood the sales process and knew that I wouldn't make any money for the first 3 months, and so I worked out how many courses per month I would need to deliver over the remaining months in order to reach my financial target. Four courses per month was all I needed. I thought "I can do this!"

However, I had no money to keep me going for the first few months so I took an evening job as a restaurant manager that paid my bills, and spent the daytimes building my business. I knew that it would be hard work but my passion was *so strong* — something I wanted more than anything — that I was not prepared to live a life without making a difference and earning money from it.

I wasn't a marketing person so I thought about all the ways I could reach potential clients, and decided to give free presentations to as many organisations as I could think of. No one turned me down.

The next step was to make follow up phone calls, my goal being to never sell on the phone, but to always arrange to meet people for coffee or at their office to connect with them at a personal level. I would find out about them, their organisation, what they wanted to achieve and their challenges and needs. Then I would discuss possible solutions that were mutually agreeable. Being real and authentic was important.

Work came in, word of mouth kicked in, and I continued to give free lunch hour teaser sessions which 20–90 people attended. Many years on I still get business from these sessions.

Of course there were challenges. I didn't enjoy making cold calls and as my evening job paid enough for me to live on, I would often procrastinate or avoid making the calls. I had two bank accounts, one for the restaurant job out of which all my bills were paid, and one for my coaching business. To stop myself procrastinating, I gave myself a good talking to and vowed to swap the bank accounts over. I knew I would, and so became more motivated to build my business. I kept my vision and my passion in front of me and kept active giving presentations, so that there was no space in my head for thoughts such as "I can't do this", "This is too hard" and "I'm not enough."

It worked. At the end of my first year I had achieved and exceeded my financial goal, earning $108,000. There were other benefits too. I got to know myself in a new way, from a depth of reality I always knew was there. I used to dream of the 'real me' and what I would be like if there were no restraints, and now I knew.

And just for the record, I still don't have a business plan, I still work from that mind map!

My advice to you would be to trust. What may hold you back is the fear of things getting too big too quickly which makes you limit what you put out there. Instead of doing ten presentations you do only four for fear of too many clients. It won't happen that way. Unleash yourself to be out there freely, fearless of whatever may come back. Trust the universe will send you only what you can handle.

Leanne is the director of two businesses: Babcock Coaching & Training and The Real You.

With an international track record, Leanne has lead transformational programmes, coached groups and individuals, and trained trainers and coaches to the level of mastery. With an impressive reputation for producing results and helping people achieve success in all areas of life, Leanne has worked with a wide range of clients from CEO's and business owners to artists and sports people, in both the public and private sectors. Her coaching is insightful, challenging, supportive and inspiring; clients typically describe it as life changing in ways they hadn't even considered possible. She has been successfully running her own business since 1993.

Monthly Life Areas check-in

Life area	Score out of 10	Notes
Family		
Physical health		
Social/Recreation		
Community		
Learning		
Spiritual		
Personal development		
Other		
Other		

CHAPTER 8   PREPARING FOR AN EXPO

You don't climb mountains without a team, you don't climb mountains without being fit, you don't climb mountains without being prepared and you don't climb mountains without balancing the risks and rewards. And you never climb a mountain on accident — it has to be intentional.

Mark Udall

I don't believe in pressure. The pressure is not being prepared for what you want to do.

Colin Kaepernick

Business expos are created to bring businesses and potential clients together. They are ways to showcase not just your product or service but you yourself. They can be very effective, profitable and inspiring but also very daunting. They are places to build trust and reputation, as well as to acquire new clients, and to make an impression. To make the *right* impression you need to be:

- Prepared
- Purposeful
- Professional
- Have a follow up process

Turning up with your wares and a few business cards is not enough. If you want to be taken seriously and be seen as a professional who knows what they are about, you need to look the part. First impressions really do count; how do the business around you look? Or more importantly, how do they compare to your stand?

Planning

- Know your audience. Who is coming? Who else is exhibiting? These are potential customers too. When you know who is coming, you know how to position your marketing and how to make your stand appeal to that audience
- Are any exhibitors likely to be competition? If so, what do you need to take into account
- Know the venue. Where is it? What does the space look like? Indoors or outdoors? How much space will you have?
- How long will you be there? How long will it take to travel there? How early will you need to arrive? Do you need to take food and drink? Something to sit on?
- What product or service are you going to present? How are you going to present it? How much do you need to take?
- What is your budget? What costs will you incur in total?
- Do you need support, an extra person to help on the day?
- Do you need power? A computer? Lighting? Payment facilities? A float?
- What will you wear? (Yes really)
- Other?

Write yourself a checklist. It could be different for each expo.

Purpose

Why are you going? What do YOU want out of the expo?

If you're not selling product, what do you want people to do? If are you a service industry do you want clients to sign up there and then or do you want to send them more information and follow up? If they say *"Yes I'm interested in that"* have a strategy in place to ensure you convert to a sale in the easiest way possible. For example, *"Great, let's book in a time now";* have a calendar ready to do that.

If you are aiming to get information out to a large group of people, just handing out flyers can be hopeful at best but what can you do after that? It makes more sense to get THEM to do something, for example enter a draw to win XXX sign up here to XXX. Then you have contact details to follow up with.

Your Stand

This needs to be attractive and clearly show who you are, what you do and why that may of interest to the passer-by. Have a banner that includes your business name and a poster that describes what your business does. The signs don't have to be flashy or expensive but they do have to be easy to read and professional.

What do you need in order to be able to display your product or service? Stands for the product? Visual aids for services? Do your research — search images online and see what others have used and what you can adapt for your business. Create a space that is interesting and appealing that draws attention.

Marketing Material

Your banners and posters are there to grab attention, but you need to give people information to take away. Business cards are still the easiest way to exchange contact details with someone; use generously and bring plenty of them.

People will be seeing a lot of stalls, so have an information sheet or flyer to hand out so they can remember your business when they get home. Remember it's about the potential customer and their needs, so your flyer shouldn't simply list all your features; instead have reasons why these might be interesting to them — the benefits. Add in a call to action too, for example "Contact me within 10 days for XXX discount", or "Let's meet for coffee and a chat".

Talking to People

Your stand is not there to just look amazing and be a decoration, it's there to attract potential customers. What are you going to do when they are arrive? Be yourself, use your networking tips, ask open ended questions.

This is where people get to know you and start building trust. How can you engage people? *"How are you today?"* immediately puts you in the unimaginative box and they will have heard it at every other stall they just passed. Try *"What brings you here?" "How are you finding the expo?"* If this part makes you anxious, create a list of questions to start conversations beforehand. Your service solves a problem — ask them if they have this problem. *"Do you have a website? What are your main issues with it?"* You can then quickly determine if they are a potential customer, and take the conversation further. If they are interested take their contact details or ask them to register online there and then, and follow up later.

Promoting Yourself

Don't leave all of this to the organisers — you want lots of people at this expo. Think about how you are going to promote yourself in the lead up as well. For instance, through blogging, social media, newsletters, networking. Reach out to your database and let them know where you will be.

Following Up

Prepare for this part before the expo. Know how you will be capturing leads, e.g. collecting business cards, names, or running a competition. Then have a process for following up. This needs to be done within a week, ideally within a couple of days. Plan an engaging email that has an offer, a proposal, or extra information. As with any contact of this kind the focus is on providing THEM with value so they want to engage further or accept an offer.

Evaluate

How do you know the expo was worthwhile? How will you measure that? For products, number of sales is a clear indication, for services this isn't as obvious. If you have collected leads you should be able to measure the conversion rate; it will just take longer to see the full effects.

In your business, those people who contact you directly should always be asked how they heard about you. This will help you understand if there are any other referrals eventuating from the expo, especially if your purpose was more about brand awareness and exposure.

What do you feel you could have done better? What worked and what didn't? Make some notes for next time.

Business expos can be very long, exhausting days with a large amount of preparation beforehand, along with follow-up afterwards, but it's important to keep up your energy and stay positive. Enjoy the conversations and find out how your business can help people. Expos are not just about sales; they're about building relationships. The networking process can be extremely rewarding.

NOTE. To make the most of this chapter: If you don't already go to expos or don't have one lined up, aim to have a stall at a business expo within three months' time (by chapter 11).

5 MINUTE MICRO-ACTIONS

- Google search "business expo image". What do and don't you like?
- Start visualising your stand
- Research any expos coming up you can attend
- Spend 5 minutes putting expo planning times into your calendar so you don't run out of time and leave everything to the last minute
- Set yourself some goals regarding preparing for an expo

GOALS

Set yourself some goals regarding preparing for an expo

Goal	Timeframe	Accountability method

RESULTS

My outcomes

NEXT STEP

NOTES

Your own notes on preparing for an expo — for example from a speaker; your own research

ANALYSIS

How would you rate yourself regarding preparing for an expo? What do you do well? What could you improve?

Monthly Life Areas check-in

Life area	Score out of 10	Notes
Family		
Physical health		
Social/Recreation		
Community		
Learning		
Spiritual		
Personal development		
Other		
Other		

CHAPTER 9   FINANCES

The people who are money-savvy … end up running the most successful businesses

Michael Gerber, Emyth

Financial freedom is available to those who learn about it and work for it

Robert Kiyosaki

Money is better than poverty, if only for financial reasons

Woody Allen

A good financial plan is a road map that shows us exactly how the choices we make today will affect our future

Alexa Von Tobel

A wise person should have money in their head, but not in their heart.

Jonathan Swift

If you don't value your time, neither will others. Stop giving away your time and talents. Value what you know & start charging for it.

Kim Garst

Financial peace isn't the acquisition of stuff. It's learning to live on less than you make, so you can give money back and have money to invest. You can't win until you do this.

Dave Ramsey

Business Numbers Made Easy

For many business owners the numbers are often a bit of mystery. When you're busy making sales, and managing stock and staff, there just isn't enough time to look at the financial stuff, let alone start to understand what all the figures mean. And it doesn't help when you ask your accountant for help and they can't explain it in plain language that you understand.

However, your ultimate success (or failure) will be measured in numbers so it's important you have at least a basic understanding of the key numbers.

Let's throw away the text book the accountants use and come up with a simple way of explaining how the numbers work in most businesses. You'll see that the key numbers are actually quite simple.

Break-even Point

- An often overlooked but vital number in business. It's the amount of sales you need to make in order to cover your costs and overheads, i.e. to avoid losses. Obviously the aim of business isn't to break-even, rather to make a profit and avoid losses; however many business owner don't know their break-even point and therefore don't set weekly/monthly sales targets to ensure they are profitable.

- If you are just starting out in business, it's critical you know the break-even point as this gives you your first target which can be broken down into a daily/weekly/monthly target to keep you focused. Your break-even point can also be used to calculate the amount of working capital (cash) you need to have available to cover expenses until sales reach the break-even trading position.

Direct Costs

- All businesses will — in the pursuit of making sales — incur 'direct' costs in creating products or services, namely labour and/or materials. These costs are often called 'variable costs' because there is a direct relationship to the level of sales or revenue made — when sales increase (or decline), then direct costs will vary up or down accordingly.

- It's vital to understand the true cost of your product or service, as this enables you to charge the right price to ensure a 'gross profit' (sales less direct costs).

Pricing

The key aim in any business is to generate sales that will allow you to make a profit after deducting both your direct and overhead costs.

If you are in an industry where prices are dictated by the market, it's vital you monitor costs regularly. Then if you detect the need to reduce prices and still want to remain profitable, you may need to reduce your costs.

It's very common for costs to creep up over time and this can quickly erode profitability if not monitored. Many businesses fall into the trap of not monitoring costs, and fail to have a process for constant small price increases to recover this cost creep.

Most reasonable people understand that you can't constantly absorb cost increases without passing them on. If you deliver a good quality product or service your customers should appreciate that you need to be profitable. Raising the subject of a price increase can be a good time to subtly remind them of why they deal with you — use it as a marketing opportunity to let them know why you're the best at what you do.

Overheads (running expenses)

- These are the expenses incurred in the day-to-day running of your business, such as rent, marketing costs, accounting fees, telephone/internet, admin wages, insurance, and power.
- Another way to look at these costs is as the expenses you incur to open the door each day, whether you sell anything or not. This is an area that can get wildly out of control, and if not monitored closely, can easily eat up your profit.
- Another type of expense that also creeps in is the 'non–business' related items and these also can blur your view of how profitable, or not, your business really is.
- If you are just starting out in business it pays to consider what your running expenses will be and factor them into your budget.

Profit Budget

- This is simply a document that sets out your future plan for sales/revenue, direct costs and overheads, so you can see how much profit you will make or lose. Not having a budget in your business is like 'flying blind', relying on hope and luck to end up with a profit.
- If you don't have any plan for your profitability, it's highly likely you will struggle to make any.
- Yes, initially completing a budget does involve quite a bit of crystal ball gazing, but the more often you complete the exercise and compare actuals against the budget, the more accurate you will become. Being able to see a trend in 3 months, rather than in 12 months when annual accounts are prepared, gives you the opportunity to arrest any adverse movement, and so is highly worth the effort.
- Profit is great, however cashflow is also vital to running a successful business. Here's more information on this side of things:

Customer (Debtor) Payments

If you give customers time or terms to pay, this can have a big impact on your cashflow. While there may be an agreement or understanding in place (Terms of Trade) about when they should pay, the reality is that not everyone sticks to it. You need to have policies and processes in place to manage every step of the way:
- the contract
- how and when you send out your invoices
- the methods of payment you provide
- how and when you follow-up arrangements for debt payment
- when you send them to the debt collector

Every dollar owed by customers is a dollar you don't have the use of; which means you have to find it from elsewhere. It may also mean delaying payments to suppliers, borrowing from the bank, or putting more of your own money into the business.

It's well known that the longer you give a customer to pay, the higher the likelihood you might lose some of the amount owed to you.

Supplier (Creditor) Payments

- The time it takes you to pay your suppliers is another opportunity for you to manage your cash so that it spends as long as possible in your bank account. However, if you give your customers terms and they take longer to pay you than you take to pay your suppliers, you will experience a cash squeeze.

- This cash squeeze is a common situation where the business owner feels uncomfortable calling overdue customers for payment, but pays suppliers straight away, because they also don't like dealing with them calling and asking for money.

- The ideal would be to have different people dealing with inward and outward cashflow, i.e. have someone who is good at calling customers with reminders to pay without getting offside, and have another person deal with supplier payments.

- The key is to have a process in place and stick to it consistently, to ensure you have a constant flow of funds.

Stock (Inventory) Control

- Stock control is probably one of the most difficult tasks faced by a business owner. One way of focusing your attention is to consider any stock on the shelves as a pile of bank notes rather than the physical item, because this highlights the value of the investment you have made while it sits on the shelf earning nothing.

- When a business carries a range of products, there is often a tendency for people to focus on the stock that's selling and neglect the stock lines that aren't selling or are slow turnover items. The result being that cash is tied up in stock that becomes unfashionable, out-of-date or obsolete, and has to be discounted to sell.

- While it's very tempting to buy when your supplier offers you a discount on extra stock, it's critical to consider the level of working capital (or overdraft) that will be tied up, and ensure that the discount will exceed the extra costs incurred for interest, storage and handling.

- The key aim if your business holds stock, is to have just enough to meet customer demand, but not so much that it sits on the shelves for too long.

Tax Payments

- While we may not like having to pay tax, unfortunately it's a fact of life. If you want to run a sustainable business you need to manage your tax obligations, such as (in New Zealand, for example) GST, PAYE and Company Tax. If you don't manage it properly the Inland Revenue will be demanding payment when you can least afford it.

- Aim to set up your tax payments in the best way to match your cashflow — monthly, quarterly or yearly.

- Some people put the tax into a separate bank account until it's due for payment, thereby separating the cash from their everyday working capital. This can avoid the situation of not having the funds available when the due date for tax payments rolls around.

Cashflow Forecast

- The cash management of a business can be quite complicated, with money coming and going, and amounts being due at certain times.
- To try and manage this without a system can be very confusing, so the best way to avoid the worry is to manage the situation with a Cashflow Forecast. This simply sets everything out in black and white.
- You can see when funds are coming in and going out, and your bank balance at any given point in the future, assuming everything goes to plan. The key is to monitor it closely and compare actual events to your forecast; then you will be in a good position to take action when things don't go as planned, to avoid running out of money.

Summary

- This information is not designed to be a technically accurate lesson in accounting, rather to highlight the key numbers you need to understand and manage in your business, to help you make a profit and manage cashflow. If you can put processes in place to manage them, it will be a great start to a sustainable and profitable business.
- As a starting point complete the 'Your Business Warrant of Fitness' on the next page.

5 MINUTE MICRO-ACTIONS

(Business Health Check-up)

Getting your financial accounts prepared monthly compared with yearly will improve your chances of survival by 50% Do you get yours prepared at least quarterly (this will improve your chance of survival by 35%)	Yes/No
Sales are Vanity, Profit is Sanity and Cashflow is Reality! Do you prepare a profit budget and monitor the actual results against the budget at least quarterly? Do you prepare a cashflow forecast and monitor the actual results against the budget at least monthly?	Yes/No Yes/No
Understanding how much you need to sell this week or hours you need to charge-out are fundamental to whether your business will survive today and into the future (ie. Your breakeven point). Do you know what your breakeven point is?	Yes/No
If you carry stock (inventory) in your business it's likely to form a major part of your business investment. When you consider the costs of holding stock, ie. storage, insurance and cost capital (Interest) this can be a great drain of profitability and cashflow. Do you undertake a stock-take more than once a year? Do you know whether your stock-turn is within industry benchmarks?	Yes/No/ NA Yes/No/ NA
It's well known amongst credit agencies, that the longer it takes a business to collect its receivables (debtors) then the greater the chance it will lose some of what's owed. Do you have a written policy detailing your 'terms of trade' Do you have documented systems to ensure the policies are being followed?	Yes/No / NA Yes/No/ NA
If your business income is derived from billing an hourly rate to your customers (clients), then keeping your rate competitive is important. However, many business owners just follow their competition rather than setting their rate to ensure they cover their costs. Have you calculated your hourly charge-out rate in the last 12 months?	Yes/No/ NA
Even though inflation is currently very low, there's a saying "if you aren't growing your business you are actually going backwards". Do you have a written plan to grow your business this year?	Yes/No

How many questions did you answer **'Yes'** (   ) and how many did you answer **'No'** (   )?

Is it time for you to complete a full Warrant of Fitness (Health Check) on your business?
Yes/No

This chapter was written by John Eaden Consulting Ltd., providing independent, affordable banking and business advice for New Zealand small to medium enterprises.

For help in calculating the break-even point; your prices or hourly charge-out rate; how to develop a profit budget or cashflow forecast for your business, or for financial training and coaching, contact john@johneaden.com, www.johneaden.com

GOALS

Set yourself some goals regarding your finances

Goal	Timeframe	Accountability method

RESULTS

My outcomes

NEXT STEP

NOTES

Your own notes on finances — for example from a speaker; your own research

ANALYSIS

How would you rate yourself regarding finances? What do you do well? What could you improve?

It's good to have money and the things that money can buy, but it's good, too, to check up once in a while and make sure that you haven't lost the things that money can't buy.
George Lorimer.

Monthly Life Areas check-in

Life area	Score out of 10	Notes
Family		
Physical health		
Social/Recreation		
Community		
Learning		
Spiritual		
Personal development		
Other		
Other		

CHAPTER 10 PRODUCTIVITY

All things will be produced in superior quantity and quality, and with greater ease, when each man works at a single occupation, in accordance with his natural gifts, and at the right moment, without meddling with anything else.

Plato

There is no such thing as work-life balance. Everything worth fighting for unbalances your life.

Alain de Botton

Sometimes we just have to suck it up and do what we have to do, until we are able to do what we want to do.

Mark W. Boyer

One of the best pieces of advice I ever got was from a horse master. He told me to go slow to go fast. I think that applies to everything in life. We live as though there aren't enough hours in the day but if we do each thing calmly and carefully we will get it done quicker and with much less stress.

Viggo Mortensen

It is not a daily increase, but a daily decrease. Hack away at the inessentials.

Bruce Lee

Too many things to do, too little time? Do you have an ever-expanding list you never get to the bottom of? Does it keep you up at night? Do you spend more time on small tasks than you should because they are easy and you are ignoring the big thing you REALLY need to get done? Are you constantly busy but still not getting what you need to get done, actually done?

You are not alone. As women we have become great multi-taskers, juggling this and that, family, life, children, jobs, building a business, fundraising etc. While you might think or feel like you are doing a lot because you are "always" busy, this is not productive, nor effective and here is why

- You make more mistakes swapping from one task to another
- It takes time to swap back from one task to another
- You aren't thinking clearly enough about the task you are working on because you are not focused enough
- You become easily distracted

In short multi-tasking is costing you in time, headspace and productivity. This is hindering your business growth not helping it.

Breathe. Take a step back. Assess how you are spending your time and what you can do to be more efficient and productive, not just busy being busy.

Plan

Create a list of tasks for the week ahead and a weekly goal that is aligned with your business strategy. Take 10 minutes every day to plan how you will spend your time by breaking it into time blocks. Blocking your time helps you stay focused on ONE task and can feel very luxurious to not have to worry about other tasks because you know you assigned them a block of their own. For example: write blog 10 -11am; create Facebook posts for the week 12 -2pm. Putting these blocks on an online calendar means you can receive notifications when it's time to change task.

Prioritise

Prioritise your tasks in order of importance. Always start with the most important tasks, before they become urgent and create stress and even less productivity, rather than the little ones you would just like ticked off your list. Staying on top of tasks keeps the panic at bay.

Automate

What can you do more efficiently by automating?

- Social media scheduling
- Canned responses for emails that are repeated

- Online payment systems such as PayPal
- Online course/workshop registration
- Automated responder emails for signups and registrations
- Automated sales process emails

Tools

Use online tools like those listed below to help with your productivity and make those little tasks more efficient.

Buffer — social media scheduling, plan your posts 2 weeks in advance.

Online calendar — such as Google for recording your time blocks.

Asana — a project management system that allows you to list your projects and the tasks associated with that project listed underneath. *For example*, 'Run Training Workshop' would have tasks like write programme, book venue etc.

Momentum — A daily to do list you can add to your desktop that asks for your daily priority so every time you open a new tab it's there keeping you on track.

Get Pocket — a tool for storing articles to read later. If you subscribe to various sites that send out industry information, you can click on *Get Pocket* and tag the article e.g. 'Marketing'; then when you want to read about marketing the info is there. You can also add a tag 'Read soon' for those times you sit with a coffee.

Capsule CRM — for managing client relationships and interaction. Set follow up tasks so you receive a daily email with a list of who to email today.

Turn off the noise

Decide when you are most productive and remove distractions. Turn off your phone, close your inbox and stay off social media.

Emails — block time when you are going to check emails and stick to it. It's OK for people to wait a few hours for an email reply. If you set good habits here it will show you exactly how much time you waste checking emails before getting back on task.

Phone — as above, we check our phones at least hourly — stop!

Social media — can be a huge time suck. You can plan your posts weekly and the have pre-determined times of day that you check in to interact with posts and groups — limit this!

Delegate

Do you really need to be doing everything yourself? There are those tasks we just keep pushing down the list and avoiding but they often create anxiety and stress which is not productive. Who can you get to help? You can potentially outsource your admin finances, sales, website etc. If you don't like doing it, there is someone else who loves it. If money is a factor think about what it will save you in terms of time and what it that is worth to you. For example it takes you 3 hours and your hourly rate is $100 per hour...doing it all yourself can be a false economy.

You won't always get everything done

Everyone in business struggles with time management — life gets in the way. There is always the unplanned, unpredicted event that just happens. Roll with it. Don't let disruption cause panic and chaos. Adjust your expectations for that time period, do what you need to do, then get back on track the next day with your planning and priorities.

5 MINUTE MICRO-ACTIONS

- Write down your to do list and prioritise
- Review what tools can help with your productivity

NOTES

Your own notes on productivity — for example from a speaker; your own research

ANALYSIS

How would you rate yourself from a productivity point of view? What do you do well? What could you improve?

GOALS

Set yourself some realistic productivity goals

Goal	Timeframe	Accountability method

RESULTS

My outcomes

NEXT STEP

Monthly Life Areas check-in

Life area	Score out of 10	Notes
Family		
Physical health		
Social/Recreation		
Community		
Learning		
Spiritual		
Personal development		
Other		
Other		

CHAPTER 11 JOINING FORCES

Be strong, be fearless, be beautiful. And believe that anything is possible when you have the right people there to support you.

Misty Copeland

The other part of outsourcing is this: it simply says where the work can be done outside better than it can be done inside, we should do it.

Alphonso Jackson

If you deprive yourself of outsourcing and your competitors do not, you're putting yourself out of business.

Lee Kuan Yew

Partnering has proven itself one of the most powerful business tools for dealing with fast changing markets, technologies and customers. As the global economy speeds up, partnering is becoming the weapon of choice for today's successful competitors.

Curtis E. Sahakian

No man (or woman) is an island — to survive and thrive in business and in life, you need to join forces with others in several ways. Don't do it all on your own!

Build a Support Network

This will be different for each person, and you'll need to work out the optimum network of people for you. Remember that we're aiming to have a fulfilling, holistic life, so taking care of both business issues and other life aspects as well, is important.

Your support network could include, for example:

- A business coach or mentor
- A life coach
- Business network group(s)
- A mastermind/peer support group
- Online groups or forums
- An informal support group

Joining a business network group can open many doors for finding others who could be in your support network. You may also benefit from finding other ways to network as well, such as working from a co-working space; attending industry-specific meetings and undertaking training programmes so that you regularly meet and get to know others. This makes it easier to ask for and provide help, gain inspiration, give and receive referrals, and more.

You may meet people who could be in a mastermind/peer mentoring group with you; a great way to help develop your business ideas. An example of how this could work is that you have a group of four people who meet monthly for two hours. Each person is allotted half an hour to explain their current business issues, and the other three provide advice and suggestions. Each person sets a monthly goal at the end of the meeting, and reports back on it at the following get-together.

If you work from home alone it's important to have strategies in place, as isolation can be a major driver for people to leave self-employment. There are now economical options such as co-working to help combat the loneliness. You could form or join an informal support group. Meeting up with others, even for coffee once a week or once a month can make a difference — you can share news, experiences, ideas, business contacts, and simply have an enjoyable time in the company of likeminded people. It may lead to social aspects as well, contributing to having a fulfilling, holistic life.

When I (Kim) gave up work in 1999 to work for myself as a writer, I found the transition from working in an office with colleagues, to working at home on my own quite a challenge, so I put an advert in the local paper asking if any "Positive, professional people" working from home wanted to form an informal support group. And so 'The Club' was born. We met weekly in a café to share laughter, news, ideas and contacts. I called it my 'sanity break', and it was a huge help to me. People came and went over the years, but I am still friends with most of the original members — which still provides me with opportunities — and The Club is still in existence.

Outsource

When starting off in a smaller business, there is a tendency to do everything yourself. Often this is driven by lack of finances. As your business progresses, it's important to make use of other resources, firstly to free you up to work on developing your business, and secondly to give a more professional slant to your business.

Delegate whenever possible; focus on what you do well and delegate the rest. Tap into the pool of resources that is available. You don't have to do everything, you don't need to know how to do everything, but you do need to know what resources are available, how to access them and how they can benefit your business.

Make use of other services by outsourcing work; for example use an accountant, bookkeeper, admin support person, designer, social media expert, copy writer, ghost writer, cold caller, and so on.

Use other support at home, such as a cleaner or a gardener.

It can often be a false economy avoiding using other services. If you can, for example, charge $100 an hour, your time may be better spent finding and undertaking work than, for example, designing your own flyer.

In addition, becoming used to doing everything yourself can become self-limiting; you might, for example, not pick up the phone to contact prospects because you are making changes to your website. Staying in your comfort zone may be comfortable, but potentially not profitable.

Benefits

- Tapping into specialised knowledge from experts in the field gives you more of a competitive advantage. It makes you more efficient. You may not have the scope of a large business but you may gain a competitive edge by outsourcing help, so you can offer the same services. If you choose people with industry expertise it can help level the playing field
- It allows you to focus on what you do — what you do well, what you want to do, and why you went into business in the first place! You can spend your valuable time on improving your products and services, and growing your business
- Outsourcing is cheaper than hiring someone

Form Business Alliances

Work with other compatible businesses to achieve better results. View other small businesses not as competitors but as collaborators — together you can achieve more. For small businesses, strategic alliances are a way to work together with others and obtain the rewards of team effort without losing your individuality. There are many forms of alliance and it us up to individual businesses to work out the format that best suits them. Alliances can be formed for different purposes, lengths of time, and at different levels of formality. They need to be aligned with the overall strategic direction of your business.

A strategic business alliance is a relationship between individuals or organisations who combine their efforts to do business together for mutual benefit. The businesses are not usually in competition, but have similar products or services they sell to similar people. You can share risk, share expenses and gain more profit. Partners may provide different things, such as products, a way to distribute goods, ability to manufacture, funding, equipment, knowledge, expertise, or intellectual property. No matter the type of alliance you choose, it is important to understand your objectives and the type of business relationship you want. Once this is decided, you can prepare the appropriate agreement — if necessary.

Potential benefits include: increased profitability; cost sharing; increased working capital and marketing/advertising budget increase; bulk order discounts; competitive advantage; elimination of competition; enhanced reputation; access to a larger/different customer base; increased visibility to other audiences; getting to market quicker; each partner can concentrate on activities that match their capabilities; gaining the knowledge of the other business's employees; increased number of strategic thinking people; larger variety of products or services; ideas sharing; enhanced problem solving; moral support.

For an alliance to be successful you need: common and agreed objectives and values; shared goals; an agreement; an understanding of, and agreement regarding roles; an understanding of the value of good finances, and the ability to manage finances well; a strong leader who can share the vision to keep people committed, build team spirit and willingness to contribute; regular, efficient meetings; a mindset of growing the alliance; a willingness to help others who may be struggling; ability to adapt to change; good communication for times when conflict arises.

As with every opportunity, there are also potential risks. For example: loss of operational control, especially if partners are not financial equals; confidentiality of proprietary information and technology; clash of corporate cultures; perceived diminishing of independence; parties may deprive themselves of future opportunities with their alliance partners' competitors.

How to set up an alliance

Step 1: Know what you are you looking for

- Work out how a strategic alliance could be useful for you: for example, to access opportunities you can't on your own; to fill gaps in your business that prevent you from growing; to meet client/customer needs that are currently not being met.
- Know the type of partner that would be beneficial for you. How could you be beneficial for them?
- Determine the workings, for example: the expected outcomes; how to protect your intellectual property; what happens if the other party/parties underperform; how to link your finances; how to assess the results of the alliance.

Step 2: Find an alliance partner(s)

Work out your criteria for an ideal partner. It should include both business and personal aspects that are important to you. Form a checklist of criteria. Make sure you know what your most important factors are and which ones would be desirable, but not necessary.

You may already know a potential partner, or you may need to find one.

Step 3: Formalise the alliance

Do you want or need a written agreement? There are different options:

- Informal. If two business owners informally agree, for example, to come together for a short-term project, to refer work to each other or bring their clients/customers together for a special event, usually a legal agreement is not necessary. Informal alliances may be agreed with a handshake
- Semi-formal. Semi-formal agreements may need a third party to look at them
- Formal. Formal agreements will need a written contract checked by a lawyer. Do your homework and have a clear understanding of what you want to achieve with your alliance prior to having the legal documents drafted

Step 4: Set up a review process

Draw up an assessment criteria checklist and organise regular times to review the alliance to see if it is working well, and what may need to be amended.

Be aware of the 'Forming, Storming, Norming, Performing' process of people working together, and analyse which stage you are at.

Understand that things may change, that you may need to be flexible and perhaps even re-format the alliance agreement.

NOTES

Your own notes on Joining Forces — for example from a speaker; your own research

ANALYSIS

How much do you do on your own? How well do your join forces with others? What could you improve?

5 MINUTE MICRO-ACTIONS

- Write a list of the synergies you could create with others
- Write down an area of your business where a business alliance could be beneficial; then write down either potential alliance partners you know, or a short list of the qualities the potential partner may need; make a note of the date/time you'll take the next step forward on this
- Decide on one activity you will delegate to someone else and either make a note of who would be possible people to delegate it to, or if you already know, send them a brief email to start the conversation

GOALS

Set yourself some realistic support goals

Goal	Timeframe	Accountability method

RESULTS

My outcomes

NEXT STEP

My outcomes

Monthly Life Areas check-in

Life area	Score out of 10	Notes
Family		
Physical health		
Social/Recreation		
Community		
Learning		
Spiritual		
Personal development		
Other		
Other		

CHAPTER 12 RECAPPING THE YEAR

Study the past if you would define the future.

Confucius

Every open and sincere evaluation of reality enhances our journey.

Joseph Rain

A truthful evaluation of yourself gives feedback for growth and success.

Brenda Johnson Padgitt

A Retrospective

Look where you have been and where you are now

How are you feeling? WOW what a journey, I'm sure there have been huge learnings along the way … but have they been the ones you expected?

Take time to read through your notes

Don't just look back and think about your journey, **read** what you were thinking along the way, follow your own journey. If you simply think about it rather than read it, you bring your current perspective, rather than seeing where you have actually been. Trust me it's worth the time, you'll learn more and gain new insight.

CHAPTER 1 GOALS

It's great — and easy — to set goals but they have a purpose and an accountability.

- Have you achieved your goals? How do you feel about your results?
- Are they still in progress? Do they need reviewing? Did your business journey help you with this?

Write down your thoughts about the goals you set at the beginning of your journey and how you feel about them now. Where they relevant; did they change along the way; did you struggle to achieve them, or did you complete them in the first few months? Did they keep you focused? What would you spend more time thinking about for your goal setting next year? What will you do differently?

Goal Setting Review

What's Next?

CHAPTER 2 NETWORKING

Throughout this year you will have had plenty of opportunity to develop your networking skills, and grow your network.

- How do you feel about networking and your networking skills now? Are you more confident and getting better results? Are you taking more opportunities to network or networking? Are you networking more in-depth?
- What has improved? What you are still working on?
- What would you like to do going forward?

Networking Review

What's Next?

CHAPTER 3 SOCIAL MEDIA

Social media is a huge minefield which hopefully you have approached with caution and purpose to achieve the results you were looking for.

- How have you navigated your social media?
- Are your social media activities achieving what you want for your business? What platforms are working for you?
- Are you spending enough time, too much or not enough time?
- Are you achieving results or just losing a lot of time?
- Does your business need social media?
- In the last six months, what ACTUAL business has social media generated for you?
- What might you need to you change?

Social Media Review

What's Next?

CHAPTER 4 MARKETING 1

Target Market; Value Proposition

This chapter's topic could have a significant impact your business. With the right market and the right messages, everything else follows.

- How easy did you find it to define your market and your value proposition?
- If you could clearly define them, how has that impacted your business? Has it made you more confident with your marketing and the way you spoke about your business? Has it resulted in higher sales?
- Are you now aiming to appeal to a wider group?
- Are you perhaps ready for a new market with a new value proposition?

Marketing 1 Review

What's Next?

CHAPTER 5 MARKETING 2

MARKETING STRATEGY

Planning your marketing takes a lot of time and focus. Looking back helps you see what your efforts have achieved for your business, and what may need adjusting.

- How is your marketing working?
- Which channels have worked best for you?
- Have you been evolving your marketing throughout the year, or did you find it better to choose a clear pathway and stay with that?
- How have you measured your return?
- Do you have numbers and $$ conversions?
- Which results are you most happy with?
- What can you improve?

Marketing 2 Review

What's Next?

CHAPTER 6 THE SALES PROCESS

Many people find sales challenging, but understanding the process of providing value and giving excellent customer service makes this much easier than you ever thought it could be. Sales are core to your business and can be extremely rewarding, both financially and otherwise.

- Have you set up a sales process?
- How are you managing it?
- Are you optimising the lead generation you achieve with your marketing?
- Have you measured your conversion rate?
- Do you feel better about sales?
- More confident?
- Is this still an area of concern for you?
- What can you do to move forward?

The Sales Process Review

What's Next?

CHAPTER 7 INSPIRATION

When we are truly inspired we can move mountains. Even small amounts of inspiration can help us take steps forward. The more open we are to being inspired, and the more we put ourselves in the right kinds of situations, the more we can experience this powerful force.

- Who and what inspired throughout the year? Why?
- What did it inspire you to do that you might not otherwise have done?
- Were you an inspiration to others? How?
- What have been the benefits?
- Could you bring more inspiration into your life?

The Inspiration Review

What's Next?

CHAPTER 8 PREPARING FOR AN EXPO

The expo has been and gone, sales, contacts and opportunities made. It may have pushed you out of your comfort zone, though hopefully it was an excellent learning experience that boosted sales and gave great business exposure.

- Were you prepared?
- Do you feel you put enough thought and preparation into this?
- Did you focus on the right things?
- Was the expo successful for you?
- Did you follow up?
- Have you worked out the return on your investment?
- What could you have done better?
- What have you learnt that would benefit you at the next event?

Preparing for an Expo Review

What's Next?

CHAPTER 9 FINANCES

Your ultimate success will be measured in numbers, so getting to grips with the key numbers to understand and manage in your business is crucial to helping you make a profit and manage cashflow.

- How has your financial management panned out over the year?
- Did you prepare financial accounts regularly?
    — Prepare and monitor profit budget and cashflow forecast?
    — Work out your break-even point?
    — Keep on top of stock and debtors?
    — Work out your charge out rate?
    — Devise a plan for growth?

Finances Review

What's Next?

CHAPTER 10   PRODUCTIVITY

Time doesn't stand still and neither does our productivity. We need to constantly work to keep this in check as life insists on throwing it out of balance. Planning, creating good habits, and using suitable tools help but it can still be a challenge.

- How are you managing your time?
- Are you happy with that?
- Have you created some good habits?
- What has helped you the most with this?
- What are your biggest challenges?
- Have you reduced your multi-tasking?
- How are you handling distractions?
- Are you taking time for yourself?
- How can you improve productivity?

Productivity Review

What's Next?

CHAPTER 11   JOINING FORCES

It's likely you will have a more successful business if you join forces with others and tap into the many benefits that working with others can bring.

- Have you found the ideal support network?
- Have you outsourced or delegated any tasks during the year?
- Have you formed any business alliances?
- Are there ways to improve on these areas?

Joining Forces Review

What's Next?

OVERALL SUMMARY

You have just reviewed the 11 chapters of your workbook and should have a good sense of all you have achieved on your journey

- What were the highlights?
- What were the low points?
- How did you move forward from that?
- How did the journey with Chrysalis help you with your business?
- How do you feel about your business overall now?
- What do you need next? What will you do next?

Overall Business Review

What's Next?

Light Bulb Moments

As you work through the workbook there will be times when you will be inspired or have an 'Aha Moment' or a wonderful idea, or the start of a wonderful idea.

This is the place where you make a note of them. Don't let those ideas slip away — write or draw them here. They may amount to nothing, they may amount to something, or they may lead to one of the greatest ideas you've ever had. And this is the page where it all started …

Light Bulb Moments

Light Bulb Moments

About the Authors

Kim Chamberlain

Kim is an international conference speaker, author of over twelve books, founder of Chrysalis for Women and real estate investor.

Through the services she provides, Kim's goal is to help people take the next step in their personal or professional development. She believes a lot can be achieved by using small periods of time regularly and effectively, and she writes and speaks on this concept.

Originally from the UK, Kim loves moving to new places, and has lived in five countries on three continents. She is married to Jon, has two children Jordan and Kira, and a very tame blue tongued called Ra. She enjoys dancing, crafts and spiritual aspects, and would refuse to be stranded on a desert island if there were no pens, paper or chocolate.

Iona Elwood-Smith

Iona is a business advisor for small to medium businesses providing affordable, practical strategies, action plans, tools and training through her company Grow My Business. She has great energy and thrives on the difference she can make to small businesses.

Having breast cancer at 40 put her on a pathway to ensure she lives life fully. She left her full-time job and set up her own business as well as joining the CanSurvive Dragon Boat team of breast cancer survivors, where she has achieved an impressive haul of national and international medals and which she now chairs.

A mother of 3 a lover of chocolate, books and pinot noir she is an advocate for women creating and living the life they want and strongly believes that to see change you need to be part of making it happen.

BOOK IONA ELWOOD-SMITH
TO HELP YOU GROW YOUR BUSINESS

Grow My Business provides affordable, practical strategies, action plans, tools, training and support for small to medium sized businesses.

Iona has extensive experience in business strategy with a strong sales and marketing background and a passion for helping businesses evolve and grow. She brings a strategic, practical perspective to business development, focusing on growth and results.

Her very practical strategies and action plans help business owners cut through the overwhelm, stay on track and put their time where it can achieve the best results.

A session with Iona is a great way to kick start your business growth. She is available on an as needed basis for regular check-ins and to walk alongside you as your business develops.

Contact Iona if you are

- too busy working in the business to grow it strategically
- wanting and needing more customers
- struggling with developing a clear business strategy
- not really sure what to do next

"Iona offers exactly what she is advertising — practical tips and tools. Every meeting we have had has been useful, actionable and Iona always follows up with next steps at the right stages. Highly recommended if you actually want to find super easy, affordable ways to grow your biz." *Ana Tomari, Eezapet.*

"Iona has been very encouraging and helpful in growing my business. At a time when I felt lost in ways to move forward, she has gave me the tools and ideas to help. Thank you!" *Carolyn Thompson, Pilates by Design*

BOOK KIM CHAMBERLAIN
TO SPEAK AT
YOUR NEXT EVENT

When it comes to choosing a professional speaker for your next event, you will find Kim Chamberlain a talented, informative, educational speaker who connects easily with audiences.

For over two decades Kim has delivered educational and inspirational presentations to audiences on several continents.

Whether your audience is 10 or 10,000, in New Zealand or overseas, Kim can deliver a customised message for your meeting or conference.

She understands that your audience will learn and be inspired — not by listening to 'theory' — but through hearing stories of inspiration, achievement, and real-life people taking steps forward in their lives.

As a result, Kim's speaking philosophy is to provide high content, easy to understand, humorous presentations that educate and inspire audiences, and she consistently receives high marks on her feedback forms.

"Kim, I was floored by your speaking ability. All conference participants mentioned you and your speech afterwards. Thank you so much for giving us some very valuable pointers about communication and motivation." *CSBM Wairarapa*

www.kimchamberlain.com
kim@kimchamberlain.com

For business development learning, networking and support

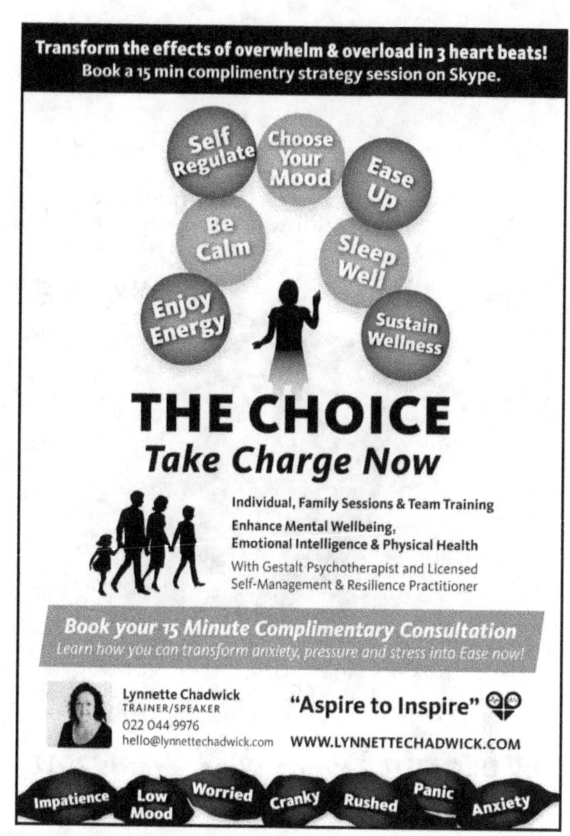

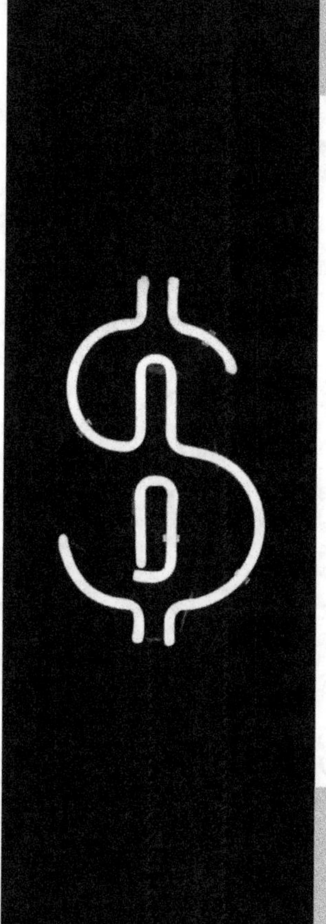

CROSS FINANCIAL SERVICES LTD

A small, friendly accounting firm based in Porirua, Wellington, specialising in individual and small business accounting and taxation matters.

If you need help working out the accounting records you need to be keeping, or the best way to set up your business, contact us for a free initial consultation.

We can guide you with all your accounting needs via paper records, excel spreadsheets, Xero, MYOB, or any other method of recording; and complete your tax return.

Gillian Cross & Joanne Ross

crossfin01@gmail.com   04 2372656